Surprised by Meaning

Surprised by Meaning

Science, Faith, and How We Make Sense of Things

ALISTER E. McGRATH

WESTMINSTER
JOHN KNOX PRESS
LOUISVILLE · KENTUCKY

First edition
Published by Westminster John Knox Press
Louisville, Kentucky

11 12 13 14 15 16 17 18 19 20—10 9 8 7 6 5 4 3 2 1

Unless otherwise indicated, Scripture quotations are from the New Revised Standard Version of the Bible, copyright © 1989 by the Division of Christian Education of the National Council of the Churches of Christ in the U.S.A., and are used by permission.

Scripture Quotations marked NIV are from the Holy Bible, New International Version. Copyright © 1973, 1978, 1984 International Bible Society. Used by permission of Zondervan Bible Publishers.

Scripture quotations marked NLT are taken from the Holy Bible, New Living Translation, copyright 1996, 2004. Used by permission of Tyndale House Publishers, Inc., Wheaton, Illinois 60189. All rights reserved.

Book design by Sharon Adams
Cover design by Lisa Buckley
Cover art © Science Faction/SuperStock

Library of Congress Cataloging-in-Publication Data

McGrath, Alister E., 1953–
  Surprised by meaning : science, faith, and how we make sense of things / Alister E. McGrath.— 1st ed.
      p. cm.
  Includes bibliographical references (p.   ).
  ISBN 978-0-664-23692-2 (alk. paper)
  1. Religion and science.   2. Meaning (Philosophy)—Religious aspects—Christianity.
I. Title.
  BL240.3.M45   2011
  261.5'5—dc22

                                                                    2010034955

Special Sales
Most Westminster John Knox Press books are available at special quantity discounts when purchased in bulk by corporations, organizations, and special-interest groups. For more information, please e-mail SpecialSales@wjkbooks.com.

Contents

Acknowledgements

This book is based on material originally prepared for the 2009 Drawbridge Lecture at King's College London; the 2009 Gifford Lectures at the University of Aberdeen, Scotland; a reflection on the relation of science and faith broadcast in Lent 2010 by the British Broadcasting Corporation (BBC); the 2010 Laing Lecture at the London School of Theology; and the 2010 Chaplaincy Lectures at Hong Kong Baptist University. I am very grateful to the original audiences for their comments, which were invaluable in reworking the material for this book.

Chapter 1

Looking for the Big Picture

Why do people like crime fiction so much? TV detectives have become an integral part of Western culture. The shelves of our bookstores are cluttered with the latest novels by the likes of Ian Rankin and Patricia Cornwell, as well as the greats from the past. Writers such as Sir Arthur Conan Doyle, Agatha Christie, Raymond Chandler, Erle Stanley Gardner, and Dorothy L. Sayers built their reputations on being able to hold their readers' interest as countless mysterious murder cases were solved before their eyes. We devour the cases of fictional detectives such as Sherlock Holmes, Philip Marlowe, Perry Mason, Lord Peter Wimsey, and Miss Jane Marple. But why do we like this sort of stuff so much?

Dorothy L. Sayers had an explanation for this. In early 1940, Sayers was invited to broadcast to the French nation, to bolster its morale in the early stages of the Second World War. She decided to boost French self-esteem by emphasizing the importance of France as a source of great literary detectives.[1] Sadly, Sayers had still not quite finished preparing her talk on 4 June 1940. The German High Command, doubtlessly realizing the window of opportunity that this delay offered them, invaded France a week later. Sayers's talk celebrating the French literary detective was never transmitted.

One of the central themes of Sayers's lecture is that detective fiction appeals to our deep yearning to make sense of what seem to some to be an unrelated series of events. Yet within those events lie the clues, the markers of significance, which can lead to the solution of the mystery. The clues need to be identified and placed in context. As Sayers put it, using an image from Greek mythology, we "follow,

1

step by step, Ariadne's thread, and finally arrive at the centre of the labyrinth."[2] Or, to draw on another image popularized by the great British philosopher of science William Whewell (1794–1866), we must find the right thread on which to string the pearls of our observations, so that they disclose their true pattern.[3]

Sayers, one of Britain's most successful and talented detective novelists, was unquestionably right in emphasizing the importance of the human longing to make sense of things. The "golden age of crime fiction," to which she was such a distinguished contributor, is a powerful witness to our yearning to discover patterns, find meaning, and uncover hidden secrets. The detective novel appeals to our implicit belief in the intrinsic rationality of the world around us and to our ability to discover its deeper patterns. We are confronted with something that needs explaining—as in one of Sherlock Holmes's best-known cases, the mysterious death of Sir Charles Baskerville. What really happened here? We were not there to observe this event. Yet by careful analysis of clues, we may identify the most likely explanation of what really happened. We need to spin a web of meaning into which this event fits, naturally and persuasively. The clues sometimes point to several possible solutions. They cannot all be right. We have to decide which is the best explanation of what is observed. Holmes's genius lies in his ability to find the best way of making sense of the clues he discovers during the course of his investigation.

We can see this human yearning to understand the enigmas and riddles of life in countless ways in our world, past and present. The Anglo-Saxons loved to tease each other with complex riddles, whose successful solution was the intellectual counterpart of proving oneself a hero in battle. More recently the rise of the natural sciences reflects a fundamental human longing to make sense of our observations of the world.[4] What greater picture unifies our disparate observations? How can the threads of evidence and observation be woven into a tapestry of truth? It is a vision that captivates the human imagination, inspiring us to long to explore and discover the deeper structures of reality.

We long to make sense of things. We yearn to see the big picture, to know the greater story, of which our own story is a small but nonetheless important part. We rightly discern the need to organize our lives around some controlling framework or narrative. The world around us seems to be studded with clues to a greater vision of life. Yet how can we join the dots to disclose a picture? What happens if we are overwhelmed with dots and cannot discern a pattern? If we cannot see the wood for the trees?

The American poet Edna St. Vincent Millay (1892–1950) spoke of "a meteoric shower of facts" raining from the sky.[5] Yet these "lie unquestioned, uncombined." They are like threads, which need to be woven into a tapestry, clues that need to be assembled to disclose the big picture. As Millay pointed out, we are overwhelmed with information, but we cannot make sense of the "shower of facts" with which we are bombarded. There seems to be "no loom to weave it into fabric." Confronted with a glut of information that we cannot process, we find ourselves living on the brink of incoherence and meaninglessness. Meaning seems to have been withheld from us—if there is any meaning to be found at all.

> We long to make sense of things. We yearn to see the big picture, to know the greater story, of which our own story is a small but nonetheless important part. Yet how can we join the dots to disclose a picture?

Many find the thought of a meaningless world to be unbearable. If there is no meaning, then there is no point in life. We live in an age when the growth of the Internet has made it easier than ever to gain access to information and accumulate knowledge. But information is not the same as meaning, nor is knowledge identical with wisdom. Many feel engulfed by a tsunami of facts, in which we can find no meaning.

This theme is developed in a profound and powerful passage in the Old Testament, in which Israel's king, Hezekiah, reflects on his experience of coming close to a complete mental breakdown (Isa. 38:9–20). He compares himself to a weaver who has been separated from his loom (v. 12). To use Millay's image that we considered earlier, we could say that Hezekiah found himself bombarded with "a meteoric shower of facts," which he could not weave together into a coherent pattern. Threads rained down on him from the heavens. But he had no means of weaving these threads together to reveal a pattern. He could not create a fabric from the threads. They seemed to be disconnected, pointing to nothing, chilling symbols of meaninglessness. The means of making sense of them has been withdrawn from him. He finds himself reduced to despondency and despair.

For some, there is no greater picture, no pattern of meaning, no deeper structure to the cosmos. What you see is what you get. This position is found in the writings of the leading atheist Richard Dawkins, who boldly and confidently declares that science offers the best answers to the meaning of life. And science tells us that there is no deeper meaning of things built into the structure of the universe. The universe has "no design, no purpose, no evil and no good, nothing but blind pitiless indifference."[6]

This is a neat, fenced-in, dogmatic creed, which offers cosy certainties to the faithful. But is Dawkins right? It seems a surprisingly superficial reading of nature, which merely skims its surface rather than looking for deeper patterns and structures. Dawkins ultimately does little more than express a prejudice against the universe possessing any meaning, even if it is dressed up somewhat unpersuasively as an argument. I suspect that the real problem for Dawkins is that he is worried that the universe might turn out to have a purpose of which he does not approve.

For most natural scientists, the sciences are to be thought of as representing an endless journey towards a deeper understanding of the world. They are simply incapable of offering slick and easy answers to the great questions of life, such as those favored by Dawkins. Forcing the sciences to answer questions which lie beyond their scope is abusing them, failing to respect their identity and their limits. Dawkins seems to treat science as if it were a predetermined atheist ideology, rather than an investigative tool through which we can gain a deeper understanding of our world.

The intellectual vitality of the natural sciences lies in their being able to say *something* without having to say *everything*. Science simply cannot answer questions about the meaning of life and should not be expected—still less, *forced*—to do so. To demand that science answer questions that lie beyond its sphere of competence is potentially to bring it into disrepute. These questions are metaphysical, not empirical. Sir Peter Medawar (1915–87), a cool-headed scientific rationalist who won the Nobel Prize in Medicine for his work on immunology, insists that the limits of science must be identified and respected. Otherwise, he argues, science will fall into disrespect, having been abused and exploited by those with ideological agendas. There are important transcendental questions "that science cannot answer, and that no conceivable advance of science would empower it to answer."[7] The kind of questions that Medawar has in mind are what some philosophers call the "ultimate questions": What are we here for? What is the point of living? These are real questions, and they are important questions. Yet they are not questions that science can legitimately answer: they lie beyond the scope of the scientific method.

Medawar is surely right. In the end, science does not provide us with the answers that most of us are seeking and cannot do so. For example, the quest for the good life has stood at the heart of human existence since the dawn of civilization. Richard Dawkins is surely right when he declares that "science has no methods for deciding what is ethical."[8] Yet this must be seen as a statement of the limits of science, not a challenge to the possibility of morality. The inability of science to disclose moral values merely causes us to move on, to search for them elsewhere, rather than to declare the quest invalid and pointless. Science is amoral. Even the atheist philosopher Bertrand Russell, perhaps one of the less-critical advocates of science as the arbiter of meaning and value, was aware of its disturbing absence of moral direction. Science, if "unwisely used," leads to tyranny and war.[9]

Science is morally impartial precisely because it is morally blind, placing itself at the service of the dictator wishing to enforce his oppressive rule though weapons of mass destruction, and likewise at the service of those wishing to heal a broken humanity through new drugs and medical procedures. We need transcendent narratives to provide us with moral guidance, social purpose, and a sense of personal identity. Though science may provide us with knowledge and information, it is powerless to confer wisdom and meaning.

So how does the Christian faith come into this? Christianity holds that there is a door hidden in the scheme of things that opens into another world: a new way of understanding, a new way of living, and a new way of hoping. Faith is a complex idea which goes far beyond simply asserting or holding that certain things are true. It is a relational idea, pointing to the capacity of God to captivate our imaginations, to excite us, to transform us, and to accompany us on the journey of life. Faith goes beyond what is logically demonstrable; yet faith is capable of rational motivation and foundation.

Faith is thus to be seen as a form of motivated or warranted belief. It is not a blind leap into the dark, but a joyful discovery of a bigger picture of things, of which we are part. It is something that elicits and invites rational assent, not something that compels it. Faith is about seeing things that others have missed, and grasping their deeper significance. It is no accident that the New Testament speaks of coming to faith in terms of the recovery of sight, seeing things more clearly, or as scales falling from someone's eyes (Mark 8:22–25; 10:46–52; Acts 9:9–19). Faith is about an enhanced capacity of vision, allowing us to see and appreciate clues that really are there, but which are overlooked or misunderstood by others.

Yet the New Testament also speaks of faith, not as a human achievement, but as something that is evoked, elicited, and sustained by God. God heals our sight, opens our eyes, and helps us to see what is really there. Faith does not contradict reason, but transcends it through a joyous divine deliverance from the cold and austere limits of human reason and logic. We are surprised and delighted by a meaning to life that we couldn't figure out for ourselves. But once we've seen it, everything makes sense and fits into place. It's like reading an Agatha Christie mystery novel already knowing the final *denouement*. Like Moses, we are led to climb Mount Nebo, and catch a glimpse of the promised land—a land that really is there, but which lies beyond our normal capacity to see, hidden by the horizon of human limitations. The framework of faith, once grasped, gives us a new way of seeing the world, and making sense of our place in the greater scheme of things.

One of the most familiar ways of envisaging God's presence in life is set out in Psalm 23, which speaks of God as our shepherd. God is always with us, a gracious and consoling presence on the journey of life, even as we "walk through the valley of the shadow of death" (23:4 NIV). The Christian tradition speaks of God as our companion and healer, one who makes sense of the puzzles and enigmas of life. The world may seem like shadowlands; yet God is our light, who illuminates our paths as we travel. As the Dominican poet Paul Murray puts it, God is "the needle's eye through which all the threads of the universe are drawn."

So how do we try to make sense of things? In the next chapter, we shall explore this in more detail.

Chapter 2

Longing to Make Sense of Things

*I*n his brilliantly argued critique of the "New Atheism," the leading British cultural critic Terry Eagleton ridicules those who think
religion was invented to explain things.[1] Eagleton has in mind the
faintly ludicrous overstatements of Christopher Hitchens on this
matter, such as his brash assertion that, since the invention of the
telescope and microscope, religion "no longer offers an explanation of anything important."[2] "Christianity was never meant to be
an explanation of anything in the first place," Eagleton retorts. "It's
rather like saying that thanks to the electric toaster, we can forget
about Chekhov." For Eagleton, believing that religion is a "botched
attempt to explain the world" is on the same intellectual level as
"seeing ballet as a botched attempt to run for a bus."

Yet despite Eagleton's correct judgement that there is far more
to Christianity than an attempt to make sense of things, Christians
do believe that certain things are true, that they may be relied upon,
and that they illuminate our perceptions, decisions, and actions. Faith
enables us to see things in different ways; it thus leads us to act in
ways consistent with this. Whatever else the Christian faith might
be, it is unquestionably concerned with believing that God exists and
that this existence possesses significance for human identity, agency,
and action. As the Harvard psychologist William James pointed out
many years ago, religious faith is basically "faith in the existence of
an unseen order of some kind in which the riddles of the natural order
may be found and explained."[3]

Christians have always held that their faith makes sense in itself
and makes sense of the enigmas and riddles of our experience. The

gospel is like an illuminating radiance that lights up the landscape of reality, allowing us to see things *as they really are*. The French philosopher and social activist Simone Weil (1909–43) made this point especially well. Although a late convert to Christianity, she came to a deep appreciation of its power to shed light on our experience of the world.

> If I light an electric torch at night out of doors, I don't judge its power by looking at the bulb, but by seeing how many objects it lights up. The brightness of a source of light is appreciated by the illumination it projects upon non-luminous objects. The value of a religious or, more generally, a spiritual way of life is appreciated by the amount of illumination thrown upon the things of this world.[4]

The ability to illuminate reality is an important measure of the reliability of a theory and is an indicator of its truth.

So how do we proceed in developing theories about reality? How do we make looms that weave threads of facts into tapestries that show patterns? How do we construct frameworks of meaning? Sometimes we inherit them from our families, or we borrow them from our friends—a sort of intellectual hand-me-down, a way of thinking that has worked for someone else, and which we hope will work for us as well. Sometimes we absorb these from our culture. Everyone else seems to believe something: so we go with the flow and believe it as well. Most people I know believe that the twenty-first century began on 1 January 2000. In fact, it began on 1 January 2001.[5] Yet nobody seems bothered about this discrepancy between popular opinion and fact.

We live in a culture in which some social assumptions and conventions seem to lie beyond challenge. However, the distinguished Polish sociologist Zygmunt Bauman wisely criticizes our tendency to trust the "prevailing ideological fashion of the day whose commonality is taken for the proof of its sense."[6] The prevalence of a belief may not be a reliable indicator of its truth, but simply a reflection of transient intellectual or cultural fashions. What seems to be permanently and globally accepted today is often discarded as an outmoded way of thinking tomorrow. Postmodernism, for example, has inverted many of the seemingly unassailable judgements of modernity, thus opening up a significant generational difference within contemporary Western thought. There's nothing wrong with critically evaluating the ideas we find around us. The problems start when we simply accept what we are told and refuse to think for ourselves.

Yet there is an alternative to passively absorbing our cultural and intellectual environments: we can develop our own way of thinking, steer our own way, and sort things out for ourselves. So how might we go about doing this? A classic approach to this question was set out by the great American philosopher Charles Sanders Peirce (1839–1914). He termed his approach "abduction," although in recent years it has become more widely known as "inference to the best explanation." It is now widely agreed to be the philosophy for investigating the world that is characteristic of the natural sciences. So how does it work?

Peirce sets out the process of thinking that leads to the development of new scientific theories or ways of thinking about reality as follows:

1. The surprising fact, C, is observed.
2. But if A were true, C would be a matter of course.
3. Hence, there is reason to suspect that A is true.[7]

Abduction is the process by which we observe certain things and then work out what intellectual framework might make sense of them. The great fictional detective Sherlock Holmes uses this same method, although he mistakenly calls it "deduction." Sometimes, Peirce suggests, abduction "comes to us like a flash, as an act of insight." Sometimes, it comes about through slow, methodical reflection as we try to generate every possibility that might make sense of what we observe.

Peirce gives close thought to how scientists develop their ideas and identifies this process as underlying the scientific method. Science begins by assembling a series of observations, then goes on to ask what framework of interpretation makes most sense of what is observed. It might be a hand-me-down, a theory borrowed from an earlier age. Or it might be a completely new way of thinking. The question that needs to be answered is this: How good is the fit between theory and observation? The phase "empirical fit" is often used to refer to this correspondence between what is seen in the world and what can be accommodated by a theory.

Consider the movements of the planets against the starry heavens. These have been observed for thousands of years. But what is the best way to make sense of them? In the Middle Ages, it was thought that the best explanation for these observations was what is often called the "Ptolemaic" model. This theory held that the earth stands at the centre of all things, and the sun, moon, and planets all revolve around the earth. It was a neat model, but by the end of the Middle Ages, it was clear that it just wasn't good enough. The observations didn't fit the theory well enough. The Ptolemaic model was groaning and creaking, unable to accommodate increasingly accurate and detailed observational evidence about the movements of the planets. It became clear that a new approach was needed. In the sixteenth century, Nicolaus Copernicus and Johannes Kepler proposed that all the planets, including the earth, rotated around the sun. This "heliocentric" model proved to be much more successful at making sense of the movements of the planets against the night sky. The close empirical fit between theory and observation suggested strongly that this theory was right. It is still the standard model adopted by astronomers.

But it's not just science that works in this way. Peirce himself was clear that lawyers also depend on abduction for their professional successes. They have to develop a theoretical lens that illuminates the evidence and brings it into sharp focus. The criminal justice system involves reaching agreement on the best explanation of the evidence laid before the courts. What is the "big picture" that makes most sense of the evidence? In the end, the theory that will persuade a jury is going to be the one that weaves as many as possible of the clues together into a coherent narrative. If there are rival ways of interpreting this evidence, the best theory is likely to be the most comprehensive, the simplest, and the most elegant. The key question before the jury is, Which is the better explanation of the evidence: the theory of the prosecution or the theory of the defence?

Here we see the quest for the big picture that makes sense of individual snapshots, the grand narrative that makes sense of individual stories, and the grand theory that connects the clues into a satisfying and coherent whole. For what applies to scientific and legal theories also applies to our attempts to make sense of life as a whole. It is as if our intellectual antennae are attuned to discern clues to purpose and meaning around us, built into the structure of the world. We need a frame of reference which helps us understand who we are, why we matter, and what we are meant to be doing.

History reinforces our appreciation of how important this quest for meaning is for human identity. Our distant ancestors studied the stars, aware that knowledge of their movements enabled them to navigate the world's oceans and predict the flooding of the Nile. Yet human interest in the night sky went far beyond questions of mere utility. Might, many wondered, these silent pinpricks of light in the velvet darkness of the heavens disclose something deeper about the origins and goals of life? Might they bear witness to a deeper moral and intellectual order of things, with which humans could align themselves? Might nature be studded and emblazoned with clues to its meanings, and human minds shaped so that these might be identified and their significance grasped? Might a longing for eternity have been planted in our hearts, to lead us home?

> Our distant ancestors studied the stars, aware that knowledge of their movements enabled them to navigate the world's oceans and predict the flooding of the Nile. Yet human interest in the night sky went far beyond questions of mere utility. Might, many wondered, these silent pinpricks of light in the velvet darkness of the heavens disclose something deeper about the origins and goals of life?

Thoughts like this have captivated the imagination of generations, from the dawn of civilization to the present day. True wisdom is about discerning the deeper structure of reality, lying beneath its surface appearance. The book of Job, one of the finest examples of the Wisdom literature of the ancient Near East, speaks of wisdom as something that is hidden deep within the earth, its true meaning hidden from a casual and superficial glance (Job 28). Wisdom is something that must be sought out; it is not found on a surface reading of nature. We cannot be content with simply skimming the surface of reality: we need to find the deeper patterns of truth lying under and behind superficial appearances. The wise are those who find a *pattern* which others have missed. As the philosopher Michael Polanyi shrewdly notes, where some people just hear a noise, others hear a tune.[8]

So why do we need these frames of reference? Why do so many people think they are so important? The answer lies partly in our quest for a reliable foundation for our lives. We all need to build our lives on the stable, solid, and secure rock of truth, rather than on the shifting sands of opinion. Yet there is a deeper issue here. Life is about more than just understanding things: it is about being able to cope with ambiguity and bewilderment, and then finding something worthwhile to give us direction and meaning. To use a phrase developed by the great British intellectual historian Sir Isaiah Berlin (1909–97), we need "thought-spectacles" to allow us to discern the complex patterns we see around us, and bring them into sharp focus.[9] But which set of spectacles allows us to see things most clearly? What picture do they disclose? And where do we fit into it?

The importance of this point was emphasized by Viktor Frankl (1905–97), whose experiences in Nazi concentration camps led him to realize the importance of discerning meaning in coping with traumatic situations.[10] Survival depends on the will to live, which in turn depends on the discernment of meaning and purpose in even the most demoralizing situations which are directly experienced as threats to survival and self-preservation. Those who cope best are those who have frameworks of meaning that enable them to accommodate their experiences within their mental maps. Frankl quotes the German philosopher Friedrich Nietzsche in making this point: the person "who has a why to live for can bear with almost any how." Frankl is speaking of the discernment of meaning, not its invention. Without the capacity to make sense of events and situations, and to attribute meaning to them, we are unable to cope with reality.

We need a mental map of reality that allows us to position ourselves, helping us to find our way along the road of life. We need a lens, a set of spectacles, which brings into clear focus the fundamental questions about human nature, the world, and God. And we need a way of checking out whether they may be trusted. Christians hold that the vision of reality granted to each of us is only a tiny fragment of a much greater truth that lies beyond us. As Paul famously remarks, "now we see in a mirror, dimly" (1 Cor. 13:12). The Christian faith declares that a reliable map exists, and that it helps us position ourselves in relation to the great questions of life. It may be a sketch-map, rather than a detailed map of the terrain. But it's good enough for our needs. We don't see the full picture in this world; but we see enough clues to know that there *is* a picture and that we are an important part of it.

So what clues might help us find this deeper level of meaning? We'll explore this question in the next chapter.

Chapter 3

Patterns on the Shore of the Universe

*T*he story is told of the ancient Greek philosopher Aristippus of Cyrene (ca. 435–ca. 356 BC), who found himself shipwrecked and washed up on the shore of the Mediterranean island of Rhodes. He had no idea of where he had landed. Was the island inhabited? As he walked along the shore, he found some geometric patterns marked out in the sand. "Let us rejoice!" he declared. "There must be people here!"[1]

Aristippus had seen features of the natural landscape which seemed to him to point to human intelligence. The patterns stood out as having been designed and drawn by people like himself. Nature itself could not have produced such structures. The only explanation that made any sense to him was that there were other people on the island.

It is a great story; yet we must not overlook its deeper significance. Aristippus observed a clue, something which he realized pointed to something else. The geometrical markings on the Rhodian sands were signs of a human presence on the island. Another story to make much the same point is Daniel Defoe's famous novel *Robinson Crusoe* (1719). Crusoe is shipwrecked on an island and believes that he is on his own. One day he is astonished to find the print of a human foot on the sandy beach. The conclusion he draws from this observation is as simple as it is inevitable: there has to be someone else on his island. He is not alone. Crusoe is not sure whether to be delighted or terrified. Is this other person a friend or an enemy? An ally or a threat?

Here we see a pattern of thinking that is particularly characteristic of the natural sciences. We observe certain things. Yet as we mull them over, we realize that they seem to point to something beyond

15

themselves—to something that is unknown and as yet unobserved. The clues in the world around us alert us to the likely existence of hitherto hidden and unknown realities. Human intellectual inquisitiveness being what it is, we long to discover these hidden truths. What we see makes us long to go beyond the horizon of our knowledge and ascertain what lies beyond. Can we discover what these clues seem to point to? Can we enter into the new world that they suggest?

> Here we see a pattern of thinking that is particularly characteristic of the natural sciences. We observe certain things. Yet as we mull them over, we realize that they seem to point to something beyond themselves—to something that is unknown and as yet unobserved.

In 1781, the British astronomer William Herschel discovered a new planet. The discovery caused great excitement since the scientific establishment of his day had assumed that there were no planets beyond those known to ancient astronomers: Mercury, Venus, Mars, Jupiter, and Saturn. After some disagreements, the international scientific community agreed to call the new planet "Uranus."[2] In the years following its discovery, astronomers watched the new planet, calculating its orbit and distance from the sun. It was immediately obvious that Uranus lies far beyond Saturn, making the solar system larger than anyone had previously thought.

Yet it soon became clear that something was wrong. By 1821 it was increasingly obvious that the new planet did not behave exactly as predicted. British and French mathematicians had calculated its orbit on the basis of the classic theory of planetary motion set out by Sir Isaac Newton in the seventeenth century. Yet Uranus did not behave as predicted. So what was the problem?

One possible explanation was that Newton's theory was wrong. Perhaps the whole theory of planetary motion would need to be revised. Perhaps the gravitational attraction of the sun does not follow Newton's predictions at such great distances. Yet there was another way of making sense of these puzzling observations. What if there was another unknown planet beyond Uranus? Its gravitational pull might distort the orbit of Uranus and make it behave in this unusual way.

Two mathematicians undertook to investigate this possibility independently. John Couch Adams in Cambridge and Urbain Le Verrier in Paris arrived at similar predictions of where a hitherto-unknown planet might be observed in the night sky. In the end, Le Verrier wrote to a colleague at the Berlin Observatory in September 1846, telling him where to look for the hypothetical new planet in the night sky. Within an hour of beginning his search, the German astronomer Johann Gottfried Galle found the planet now known as "Neptune."[3]

This well-known story is often told to emphasize the predictive power of the natural sciences. Science does often get things wrong, making predictions that turn out to be based on incorrect assumptions. Yet even these failures are instructive. After all, they help identify false assumptions and force their correction. Adams and Le Verrier were confident that the puzzling behaviour of Uranus was only perplexing because it was being interpreted against the wrong background. Using one theoretical lens, it was opaque and out of focus. But they were confident that another theoretical lens could be found which would bring its behaviour into sharp focus, casting light on the celestial movements and offering an explanation of why Uranus behaved in this way. And as events proved, that confidence proved justified.

Here we see the classical outline of the scientific attempt to make sense of our observations of the world. Things don't just *happen*. They fit into a pattern, a bigger picture, an overall scheme of things. What theory makes most sense of what we experience and observe in the world? The need to "preserve the phenomena" in scientific explanation has been appreciated since the time of Aristotle, in the classical era. Scientific theories change over time for two main reasons. First, new discoveries are made, which mean existing ways of thinking have to be re-evaluated. Second, a new theory is developed which makes better sense of the observational evidence than existing theories.

The new explanation of the mysterious orbital behaviour of the planet Uranus was easily checked out and shown to be right. But things are not always that straightforward. Sometimes a theory seems to make a lot of sense of what is observed; yet it cannot be *proved*, because there just isn't enough information available. A classic example of this is Charles Darwin's theory of natural selection, set forward in his *Origin of Species* (1859).

Darwin was faced with a series of observations about the natural world which he believed did not fit well into existing theories of the origin of species. For example, why did some species have vestigial structures: such as the nipples of male mammals? Darwin believed that his own theory of natural selection made more sense of these observations than any other theory. But he could not *prove* it was right. There were loose ends everywhere. His theory cast light on many observations of the natural world—but not all of them. Darwin was nevertheless convinced that his theory was right. It was just too good to be false: it explained so many things and explained them so well.

> It can hardly be supposed that a false theory would explain, in so satisfactory a manner as does the theory of natural selection, the several large classes of facts above specified. It has recently been objected that this is an unsafe method of arguing; but it is a method used in judging the common events of life, and has often been used by the greatest natural philosophers.[4]

The point that Darwin was making was simple and is not scientifically controversial. Only in rare cases can a scientific theory be proved to be true beyond all doubt. In most cases, theories are accepted as true because they make enough sense of things to persuade us to take them seriously. Although some recent atheist writers have suggested that Darwin limited his view of reality to what could be *proved*, Darwin was quite clear that many scientific theories had to be accepted on faith and in trust. Darwin was a champion of scientific inquiry, not of dogmatic atheism. Darwin was convinced that there would always be an element of doubt in a theory which offered such a "big picture" of things. Not everything was a perfect fit. But his theory of natural selection accommodated many things so well that its truth seemed assured, despite anomalies, apparent contradictions, and some evidence that just didn't seem to fit in with the theory.

> A crowd of difficulties will have occurred to the reader. Some of them are so grave that to this day I can never reflect on them without being staggered; but, to the best of my judgment, the greater number are only apparent, and those that are real are not, I think, fatal to my theory.[5]

The capacity of his theory to explain, in Darwin's view, was a reliable indicator of its truth.

Not everyone was persuaded.[6] There were too many theoretical and evidential loose ends, they argued. Many of these were sorted out in the ensuing decades, when some of the difficulties Darwin had noted turned out not to be such problems after all. But Darwin believed that he didn't need to wait for all the loose ends to be tied up or for every aspect of his theory to be confirmed. His theory was just too good at explaining things for it to be wrong.[7]

That's what most scientists think. Darwin is not an exception: in many ways he is a model of scientific thinking, now often expressed in terms of "inference to the best explanation." Some of Darwin's ideas are echoed in the famous essay "The Sentiment of Rationality" by the psychologist William James (1842–1910), who argues that human beings all need what he calls "working hypotheses" to make sense of our experience of the world.[8] These "working hypotheses" often lie beyond total proof, yet they are accepted and acted upon because they are found to offer reliable and satisfying standpoints from which to engage the real world. For James, faith is a particular form of belief, which is pervasive in everyday life. James understands faith as "belief in something concerning which doubt is still theoretically possible." Taking this idea a stage further, James declares that "faith is synonymous with working hypothesis." We hold that certain things are true, and we rely upon them—while realizing that we cannot prove them to be true in the way that we could prove a proposition from Euclid's geometry.

James thus affirms the possibility of believing in a theory, a way of making sense of things, a "working hypothesis," which is not finally confirmed and may not ultimately be capable of final confirmation—yet which is found to be reliable. Darwin's theory is an excellent example of the kind of thing that James has in mind. But James's idea of a "working hypothesis" goes far beyond Darwin's theory of natural selection as an explanation of the natural world, and beyond any other scientific theory. It concerns one of the most profound realities of human existence: things that are really worth believing in lie beyond proof. Our most important beliefs are the ones that simply cannot be proved.

This is an unsettling point, one that needs closer attention. There are a number of statements that can be proved beyond doubt. Here are three of them:

1. $2 + 2 = 4$.
2. The whole is greater than the part.
3. The chemical formula for water is H_2O.

While these are all true, none of them can exactly be said to give us a reason for living. None gives us reason to wake up in the morning with a song in our heart or a sense of purpose in our lives.

Christians believe that there is a God, whose loving presence and grace transform human nature and give us a reason to live and to hope. It cannot be proved. But it is a belief which, if true, utterly transforms life. We see everything in a new way and a new light. The atheist believes that there is no God. This article of faith cannot be proved either. Christianity and atheism are both faiths, what William James calls "working hypotheses." They are of critical importance to people's lives. But they can't be proved.

I recall a conversation with an atheist in London after a debate. He was a very courteous and gracious person, who explained to me that he did not believe in God and did not believe he needed to believe in God. What gave his life purpose, he told me, was the goodness of human nature. Without this philosophical and moral lodestar, his life would have no purpose. I told him that my belief in God was a bit like that. He smiled and shook his head. "I have no need for faith," he told me. I pointed out, in what I hope was a gracious and kindly manner, that as a matter of fact he *did* have faith. Whether he liked it or not, he had faith in the goodness of human nature. I explained that it was not a faith that I felt I could share with him. And I told him why. I spoke of the profound ambiguity of human nature and the horrors that human beings inflicted on each other. I spoke of Auschwitz and nuclear weapons. I just couldn't share his faith. There was too much evidence against it. Maybe we are capable of doing good; but we also seem to be capable of doing evil. I couldn't share his belief in the goodness of human nature. It didn't square with the evidence.

My friend—I hope I can call him that—paled. We talked a bit more. I pointed out how I and many others believed that democracy was better than fascism, that liberty was better than oppression.

These were passionate and deeply moral beliefs. Yet they could not be proved to be true. So, I asked my friend, was I wrong to hold them? No, he replied, adding that he believed these things himself. As we prepared to go our separate ways, I left him with the thought that the things that really matter in life are ultimately matters of faith. They can't be proved. But we continue to believe in them, and we are justified in doing so. That's just the way things are. His final words to me as we parted were simple: "I've got some thinking to do."

One of the more puzzling features of the New Atheism is its aversion to any suggestion that atheists have beliefs. Yet we all do. That's the way we are. To believe is human. That doesn't stop us from trying to work out which beliefs are most reliable. So how do we make sense of things and come to a reliable judgement about the best frame of reference? We will explore this further in what follows.

Chapter 4

How We Make Sense of Things

Science is about sense-making. The natural sciences try to identify patterns within the natural world and then to seek out the deeper structures which can account for these patterns:

> The hallmark of natural philosophy is its stress on *intelligibility*: it takes natural phenomena and tries to account for them in ways that not only hold together logically, but also rest on ideas and assumptions that seem right, that make sense.[1]

Michael Polanyi, the Hungarian chemist who later went on to explore the philosophical implications and consequences of the scientific method, neatly summarizes the dynamics of the scientific endeavour: "The pursuit of discovery," he writes, is "guided by sensing the presence of a hidden reality toward which our clues are pointing."[2]

We observe things on the surface of reality and try to work out their deeper structures. The great scientific pioneer Isaac Newton (1643–1727) came to realize that there was a common "hidden reality" lying behind the motions of bodies on earth, such as the falling of an apple from a tree, and the movement of the planets round the sun. Newton called this invisible, intangible, hidden reality "gravity" and was never quite sure that the notion actually made sense. His explanation of things seemed to raise as many questions as it answered. As history records, a gallery of hecklers protested against this idea of an invisible, intangible, unobservable force. But Newton was clear that it seemed to be the best way of explaining what he observed. The existence of gravity is now taken for granted, as part of the furniture of the scientific worldview.

Science, therefore, can be thought of as a quest for what Polanyi called "a hidden reality toward which our clues are pointing." Here the use of the word "clue" is very significant because it points immediately to a degree of uncertainty in our knowledge. We observe certain things; but what is their meaning? C. S. Lewis famously described things such as the human sense of right and wrong as "clues to the meaning of the universe." Such "clues" are not hard proofs: they are soft pointers. Yet the accumulation of such clues often has an intellectual intensity that transcends the power of some so-called proofs.

Scientific explanation can be thought of as the quest for a "hidden reality," a deeper structure, which makes sense of our observations and experiences of the world. So how might this "deeper structure" explain anything? Three major understandings of scientific explanation are widely used in the philosophy of science:

> We observe certain things; but what is their meaning? C. S. Lewis famously described things such as the human sense of right and wrong as "clues to the meaning of the universe." Such "clues" are not hard proofs: they are soft pointers.

1. Explanation as the identification of causes.[3]
2. The identification of the "best explanation," which makes most sense of what we observe.[4]
3. "Explanatory unification," which establishes a common framework for what were once thought to be unrelated events.[5]

We will explore each of these approaches in a little more detail and consider how they illuminate the human quest to make sense of things.

1. Causal Explanation

The most familiar type of explanation is causal. If A causes B, then A explains B. It is an idea that is familiar to everyone. If I throw a hardball at a neighbour's window and it breaks, then my action is an explanation of why the window broke. Causal explanations play a major role in science. In the debate now raging about global warming, the key question is whether human beings have caused environmental changes through the production of greenhouse gases. If the world is getting warmer, how is this to be explained? Identification of the causes of global warming is essential if the trend is to be checked, let alone reversed.

But what about more difficult questions? For example, how are we to explain the origins of the universe? Was the universe caused by something or someone? The old idea of the eternity of the universe, characteristic of much earlier science, has now generally been abandoned, on account of increasing evidence that the universe had a beginning. The twentieth century saw dramatic changes in our understanding of the origins and development of the universe.[6] Its first two decades were dominated by the assumption that the universe was static. Yet during the 1920s, evidence began to emerge suggesting that the universe was indeed expanding. Up to this point, it had been generally (though not universally) assumed that the nebulae observed in the night sky—such as M31 in Andromeda, or M42 in Orion—were part of the Milky Way, the galaxy within which our solar system is located. On the basis of observations at the newly constructed 100-inch telescope at the observatory on Mount Wilson, a peak in the San Gabriel mountains in California, Edwin Hubble (1889–1953) proposed that these objects were galaxies in their own right, lying far beyond our own. By developing work on the spectral redshifts of these galaxies, Hubble was able to propose that the greater the distance between any two galaxies, the greater their relative speed of separation. The universe was expanding, with increasing speed, and apparently irreversibly.

In Hubble's time, it was a difficult idea to accept since it seemed to suggest that the universe must have evolved from a very dense initial state: in other words, it implied that the universe had a beginning. But this was merely a suggestion, one way of making sense of the observations. Other ways of making sense of astronomical observations were certainly possible. The best known of these was set out in 1948, when Fred Hoyle and others developed a steady state theory of the universe, which held that the universe, although expanding, could not be said to have had a beginning. Matter was thus being continuously created in order to fill in the voids arising from cosmic expansion.

Opinion began to shift in the 1960s, chiefly on account of the discovery of the cosmic background radiation by Arno Penzias and Robert Wilson at the Bell Laboratories in New Jersey.[7] They were experiencing some difficulties: irrespective of the direction in which they pointed their antenna, they found that they picked up an unwanted and obtrusive background hissing noise which they simply could not eliminate.

It was only a matter of time before the full significance of this irritating background hiss was appreciated. It could be understood as the "afterglow" of a primal cosmic explosion—a hot big bang— which had been proposed in 1948 by Ralph Alpher and Robert Herman. This thermal radiation corresponded to photons moving about randomly in space, without any discernible source, at a temperature of 2.7 K (on the Kelvin scale). Taken alongside other pieces of evidence, this background radiation points to the inescapable conclusion that the universe had a beginning, and it caused severe difficulties for the rival steady state theory.[8]

Since then, the basic elements of the standard cosmological model have become clarified and have secured widespread support within the scientific community. Although there remain significant areas of debate, this model is widely agreed to offer the best resonance with observational evidence. The universe is now believed to have originated some 14 billion years ago and to have been expanding and cooling ever since. The standard cosmological model, often referred to as the "big bang," describes a universe which is not eternal, but which came into being a finite time ago from nothing.[9] So what has caused it to appear? Perhaps the cosmos created itself. Perhaps it just happened. Or perhaps it was brought into creation by an agent—such as God. The traditional Christian doctrine of creation from nothing (ex nihilo) has enjoyed a new lease of life as a result of the new insights.[10] Might the characteristics of the world, such as its ordering, reflect its divine origins? We shall return to consider this point later.

This kind of approach to scientific explanation can easily be used to assert the rationality of the Christian faith, by arguing for the necessity of God as an explanation of the existence of the universe. Many traditional arguments for the existence of God treat God as an agent who intentionally brings about certain phenomena which are observed to take place. The philosopher of religion William Lane

Craig, for example, deduces the existence of God in this way, using the following type of argument:

1. We have good reasons, philosophically and scientifically, to believe that the universe is not eternal, but had an absolute beginning.
2. But something cannot come into being out of nothing.
3. Therefore, there must be a transcendent cause of the origin of the universe—which is God.[11]

Many atheistic cosmologists initially opposed the idea of the big bang, arguing that, if there was a beginning, then there must be a beginner. It was an embarrassing conclusion to have to draw, but the science increasingly seemed to point in that direction.

2. The Best Explanation

The second approach to scientific explanation recognizes that there will always be multiple interpretations of our observations and experiences. But which is the best? Often the evidence is not good enough to allow us to reach a clear and certain decision. Yet this does not mean that we have to throw up our hands in despair and declare that all interpretations are equally good (or bad). Charles Darwin, for example, was aware that his theory of natural selection was only one of several possible explanations of the features of the biological world. His theory faced competition from the "transformist" idea of the gradual development of species over time.[12] Yet he still believed that he was justified in declaring that his theory was the best explanation and that it would eventually be shown to be the best explanation.

So how might rival theories be judged? How do we determine which is the best? The core idea here is "empirical adequacy": the measure of how well a theory accounts for what is actually observed. How well does the theory map onto the world of experience? How good is the fit between theory and observation? The "best" explanation may not be able to account for all our observations. But it ought to be able to account for them to a greater extent, and in a more plausible manner, than its alternatives.

Nor can the "best explanation" always be proved to be right. Often it must be accepted on trust, as the best way of making sense that is available to us. Science is thus about motivated or warranted belief: something that we believe to be true and believe to be justified in believing, while we know that it cannot always be proved. As we noted earlier, Darwin was clear that his theory of natural selection could not be proved. Nevertheless, it remained the best explanation of what was observed, and it deserved to be regarded as correct on that basis. "The change of species cannot be directly proved," Darwin wrote, so that "the doctrine must sink or swim according as it groups and explains phenomena."[13] In other words, we have to ask how successful a theory is at making sense of the world, while we look over our shoulder at its rivals.

Finally, the "best" explanation may not be the most reasonable or commonsense explanation. Scientists don't lay down in advance what is reasonable. Time and time again, they have found the natural world to contradict what common sense might have expected or predicted. Science would fail if it were forced to conform to human ideas of rationality. Quantum theory is a classic example of a scientific field which seems to fly in the face of human reason, offering an account of the quantum world which seems totally counterintuitive. "The instinctive question for the scientist to ask is not 'Is it reasonable?' as if one knew beforehand the shape that rationality had to take, but 'What makes you think that might be the case?'"[14] Science is about *warranted* belief, not about *rational* belief. The history of science is about the recalibration of notions of "rationality" in the light of what was actually discovered about the deeper structure of nature.

3. Explanatory Unification

The third approach to scientific explanation is based on the idea of "unification." This involves establishing connections between ideas that were once thought to be unrelated, so that they can now be seen as different aspects of the same big picture. A good example of this is found in the writings of the Scottish physicist James Clerk Maxwell (1831–79), who published a unifying theory of electricity and magnetism in 1865. This theory demonstrates that electricity and magnetism are like the two sides of the same coin. The unification of explanation can also be seen in Descartes's unification of algebra and geometry, Isaac Newton's unification of terrestrial and celestial theories of motion, and Einstein's demonstration of the unity of physics. Not all attempts to achieve unification have been successful; to date, for example, the unification of quantum and relativity theory still remains a distant goal.

The famous quest for the "theory of everything" can be seen as another classic example of this approach. This theory, once it is discovered (though some believe it lies beyond our reach), is expected to provide a framework of meaning that will allow every other theory to slot neatly into its allotted place. Unificatory explanation is the search for the big picture, the grand map, which allows everything to be seen in its proper relationship.

On this approach to scientific explanation, the big question concerns the trustworthiness and capaciousness of theoretical panoramas. What theory of reality accounts both for observation on the one hand, and successful theories on the other? How good is it at interweaving and interlocking what we know about the universe? Such a unified understanding of the world will aim to be both *economic* (making as few assumptions as possible) and *extensive* (embracing as much as possible of what we know about the world).

These three approaches to scientific understanding are not inconsistent with each other. They clearly overlap at points, even if their emphases are subtly different. It is important, for example, to realize that not all explanations are causal. Furthermore, the process of explanation is often regressive, leading to the question of whether there is an ultimate explanation of all things, or whether there exists an infinite chain of explanations. The quest for a theory of everything or a grand unified theory can be seen as an attempt to offer a comprehensive explanation of explanations, driven by the desire to have as comprehensive and unified an understanding of reality as possible.

Yet in recent years, it has become increasingly clear that science is raising questions which it cannot answer. Questions arise out of the scientific understanding of the world which seem to direct us beyond science itself, pointing towards a deeper level of intelligibility. Is there something beyond science which helps us make sense of both the successes and limits of science? Might there be a deeper order of things, in which the riddles and enigmas of human existence might find their resolution?

This book will explore one answer—an answer beautifully hinted at in a phrase in the writings of the distinguished Canadian philosopher Bernard Lonergan (1904–84): "God is the unrestricted act of understanding, the eternal rapture glimpsed in every Archimedean cry of Eureka."[15] But first, we must consider the recent emergence of a movement that has denied any such notion, almost as a matter of principle: the New Atheism.

Chapter 5

Musings of a Lapsed Atheist

*T*he New Atheism made its dramatic appearance over the period 2006–2007, topping bestseller charts and provoking a huge and often highly charged public debate over the rational basis of faith and the place of religion in contemporary life. The leading representatives of this movement—Richard Dawkins, Sam Harris, Daniel Dennett, and Christopher Hitchens—offer an aggressive, blistering attack on religion.[1] Like the Italian army major in Ernest Hemingway's *Farewell to Arms* (1929), they are adamant that "all thinking men are atheists."[2] While the New Atheism is light on rigorous evidential analysis, often asserting opinions as if they were facts, it excels in the use of rhetoric. Religion is portrayed as being intrinsically and characteristically dangerous, poisonous, and evil. There is no allowance that religion might have even one or two redeeming features. This aggressive and dismissive approach resonates deeply, perhaps at a sub-rational level, with the fears of many secularists in Western culture. Lurking within every religious believer there lies a potential terrorist. Get rid of religion, and the world will be a safer place.

Why the intense anger? Part of the explanation lies in the refusal of religion to die out in the West, as the great secularists of the recent past predicted. Back in the 1960s, when I was growing up, part of the received wisdom of the age was that religion was on its way out. As a social influence, its days were numbered; as a credible worldview, it was a "dead time's exploded dream" (Matthew Arnold). Its stubborn persistence and continuing influence, especially in the United States, has alarmed atheists and secularists. A good example of this concern is found in a short speech given in 2006 by the anti-religious writer Ian McEwan, to mark the thirtieth anniversary of the publication of Richard Dawkins's *The Selfish Gene*.[3] McEwan speaks of his surprise and dismay at the resurgence of religion, and he argues that there is an urgent need to put it back into its proper place—which, for McEwan, is in the private thoughts of backward individuals, kept safely away from any public places.

I used to think that as well. During the late 1960s, a surge of secularist euphoria swept across Western Europe and North America. In April 1966, *Time* magazine's cover story was the death of God. Sociologists were predicting the dawn of a new secular era, in which belief in God would die out and be replaced by secular ideologies, such as Marxism. A tidal wave of anti-religious feeling was sweeping across the face of Western culture. The commentator and novelist Tom Wolfe caught this cultural mood well in his essay "The Great Relearning," based on his experiences in San Francisco in 1968. Everything was to be swept aside in a frenzy of dissatisfaction and rebuilt from ground zero.[4] Never before had such a radical Promethean reconstruction of things been possible. It was time to seize the moment and break decisively with the past! Religion would be swept aside as the moral detritus of humanity, at best an irrelevance to real life, and at worse an evil, perverse force which enslaved humanity through its lies and delusions.

That was the cultural mood of the late 1960s. And I shared it. Everyone likes to feel that they are somehow connected with the great stories of history, and I came to see myself as part of this anti-religious vanguard. Marxism was the oxygen of the cultural atmosphere of the day throughout much of Western Europe at this time, even in my own native Northern Ireland. Yet for me, the Marxist critique of religion was supplemented by something just as powerful and persuasive: the scientific view of reality.

Science explained everything. It gobbled up the conceptual space once occupied by God and replaced it with the sane, cool rationalism of the scientific method. Only scientific claims are meaningful. Anything that lies outside the scope of science is simply superstition or delusion, no matter how understandable. The sciences were, for me, the bright lodestar of my intellectual and moral endeavours, the only true way to acquire reliable knowledge about reality and the order of things. Atheism was my creed, and science was its foundation.

I won a scholarship to Oxford University to study chemistry, seeing this as both immensely satisfying in its own right and also as a
means of consolidating and extending my atheism. While preparing
to go up to Oxford, however, I began to read works dealing with the
history and philosophy of science. This turned out to be a baptism
of fire. My mind was assaulted with ideas that battered at the roots
of my faith. I read about the under-determination of theory by data,
and radical theory change in the history of science. I was forced to
confront the difficulties in devising a "crucial experiment," and the
enormously complex issues associated with determining what was
the best explanation of a given set of observations.

The seeds of doubt were planted in my mind. Was my atheism
really some kind of logical fallacy based on a misunderstanding of
the proper scope of science, or a misunderstanding of the nature of
scientific claims? It was a deeply unsettling thought, and I tried not
to think about it too much. Nobody likes their personal worlds of
meaning to be disturbed too much. I was tempted to dismiss this sort
of stuff in much the same way that Dawkins still does—as ignorant,
unscientific "truth-heckling."[5] But my doubts would not go away.

When I arrived at Oxford, I decided to look into these things properly, to set my mind at rest. I expected to find my atheism reinforced
so that I could dismiss such intellectual distractions. I wanted closure
of this question so that I could get on with more important things.
Yet while I had been severely critical of Christianity, I realized that I
had yet to extend that same critical evaluation to atheism, tending to
assume that it was self-evidently correct and hence was exempt from
being assessed in this way. During October and November 1971, I
began to discover that the intellectual case for atheism was rather
less substantial than I had supposed. Far from being self-evidently
true, it seemed to rest on rather shaky foundations. Christianity, on
the other hand, turned out to be far more robust intellectually than I
had supposed.

Finally I realized that atheism was actually a belief system,
although I had assumed it to be a factual statement about reality. In
the end, I turned my back on one faith and embraced another. I turned
away from one belief system that tried to deny it was anything of the
sort, and accepted another which was quite open and honest about its
status. My conversion was an act of free-thinking. I believed that I

had found the best way of making sense of things. And that remains my view today. Although I now appreciate that Christianity has emotional, imaginative, and ethical dimensions that I had yet to discover at that time, I continue to see the "sense-making" dimensions of faith to be profoundly important and significant.

When I first read the leading works of New Atheism of 2006–2007, my initial reaction was one of deep nostalgia. I found myself smiling at the bold, aggressive, and dismissive declarations of the evils of religion and the delusion of faith. It reminded me of my own youth, when I used to share both these beliefs, and the arrogance which arose from them. Yet what interested me most was the way in which so many of the New Atheist writers made the natural sciences a core element of their atheistic apologetics.

The New Atheism frequently makes a rhetorical appeal to the natural sciences as the sole basis of reliable truth—a view now widely known as "scientism"[6]—and the concomitant rejection of religious belief as evidence-free superstition. On this view, science demands no commitments of faith; in fact, its emphasis on truth is the enemy of faith. The critical role of fiduciary judgements in the scientific method is simply airbrushed out of the picture.[7] Although this theme is rhetorically echoed in the works of Harris and Hitchens, it finds its fullest discussion in the works of Dawkins and Dennett.

Curiously, Dawkins and Dennett remain firmly committed to the outmoded notion that science and religion are permanently in conflict—an idea often referred to as the "warfare" thesis. This is now regarded as quite unacceptable by historians of science, chiefly because it is so difficult to reconcile with the facts of history.[8] It is one of many points at which the "New Atheism" is seriously out of line with modern scholarship. The idea that science and religion are in a state of permanent conflict became highly popular in the late nineteenth century, largely for sociological reasons. Though it remains persistent in the popular media, it has lost scholarly support as a result of our growing knowledge of the historical interactions of science and religion. Yet Dawkins is so unswervingly committed to this obsolete warfare model that he has been led to make some very unwise and indefensible judgements. One of the most foolish of these is the ridiculous idea that scientists who promote a positive working relationship between science and religion can be compared to the British prime minister Neville Chamberlain in his attempt to appease Adolf Hitler.[9] It is a bizarre suggestion, to be set alongside Dawkins's more recent assertion that creationism is comparable in its intellectual and moral depravity to Holocaust denial.[10] The derision with which this suggestion has been greeted suggests that the New Atheism sometimes seems to occupy a fantasy world, isolated from the real world around it.

> The idea that science and religion were in a state of permanent conflict became highly popular in the late nineteenth century, largely for sociological reasons. Though it remains persistent in the popular media, it has lost scholarly support as a result of our growing knowledge of the historical interactions of science and religion.

One of the central themes developed by both Dawkins and Dennett is that Darwinism is a universal theory, capable of explaining far more than developments within the biological realm. Religion, both argue, can be accounted for within a Darwinian context. It is easily understood as an "accidental by-product" or a "misfiring of something useful."[11] So why does Dawkins believe that religion can be explained in terms of a Darwinian model? Dawkins's analysis rests on the "general principles" of religion that he finds in Sir James Frazer's *Golden Bough*—a highly impressionistic early work of anthropology, first published in 1890. At first sight, this seems to be a highly puzzling strategy. Why would Dawkins make his theory of the origins of religion depend so heavily on the core assumptions of a work which is well over a century old, and now largely discredited? Isn't he meant to be bringing things up to date, rather than lurching back into the past, digging up old and discredited approaches?

Yet it soon becomes clear that Dawkins depends upon Frazer's theory of religion to make his case. Frazer's insistence that religion may be reduced to some single universal trait opens the door for Dawkins to propose a Darwinian explanation. By presenting religion as something that possesses universal characteristics, it is open to Darwinian analysis, and hence to reductive explanation. "Universal features of a species demand a Darwinian explanation."[12]

Most anthropologists now cite Frazer as an example of how *not* to study religion. Religion does not exhibit the "universal features" that Dawkins's preferred approach demands, and which late Victorian works of the anthropology of religion erroneously regarded as axiomatic. Frazer's strategic assumption of "the essential similarity of man's chief wants everywhere and at all times" may suit Dawkins's anti-religious agenda, but it does not fit the facts.

It may initially seem puzzling that *The God Delusion* depends on discarded nineteenth-century assumptions to make a twenty-first-century case against religion.[13] But the reason soon becomes painfully obvious: when care is taken to define "religion," it turns out not to fit the simplistic categories upon which Dawkins's analysis depends. Religion clearly belongs to what the philosopher Donald Brown calls "universals of classification" rather than to "universals of content."[14] "Universals of content" have shared core beliefs; "universals of classification," on the other hand, share common patterns, but not necessarily individual beliefs. They have fuzzy boundaries and lack easily distinguishable core convictions.

Both Dawkins and Dennett believe that the natural sciences exclude metaphysical commitments, especially of a religious nature, holding that these are ultimately spurious. Yet when properly and legitimately applied, the scientific method is religiously neutral—neither uniformly supportive nor uniformly critical of religious beliefs. Since the scientific method clearly does not entail atheism, those who wish to exploit the sciences as a weapon against religion have to supplement their case in certain ways to increase its plausibility. One way is by using aggressive rhetoric, heaping ridicule on those who challenge its obvious inaccuracies. Another way is to rewrite the narrative of science, incorporating atheistic presuppositions into the narrative of the scientific method.

Dawkins is a master of smuggling metaphysics into science, rewriting the neutral and often inconclusive scientific narrative so that it leads to a rigorous atheist conclusion. The way in which he imposes an atheistic meta-narrative on a scientific description of things can be explored by examining a passage from Dawkins's early masterpiece *The Selfish Gene* (1976). This supplements overt scientific description with a covert metaphysic which represents genes as active agents in control of their own destiny and the destinies of their hosts:

> [Genes] swarm in huge colonies, safe inside gigantic lumbering robots, sealed off from the outside world, communicating with it by tortuous indirect routes, manipulating it by remote control. They are in you and me; they created us, body and mind; and their preservation is the ultimate rationale for our existence.[15]

This passage presents a completely defensible scientific statement—"genes are in you and me"—with a series of equally indefensible metaphysical assertions. We are told, for example, that the preservation of our genes "is the ultimate rationale for our existence." A scientifically illiterate reader of this passage might assume that Dawkins was providing an answer to the age-old question of the meaning of life. On this reading of things, the reason for existence is the preservation of our genes.

This is, however, simply a presentation of a "gene's-eye view"—a hypothetical metaphysical way of interpreting scientific observation. This approach, which arguably reached its zenith in the early 1980s,[16] conceived of the gene as an active controlling agent, which could be regarded as "manipulating" the destiny of biological entities, including humanity. Yet the empirically verified facts in this statement are limited to the brief statement that genes "are in you and me." The rest is speculative. Metaphysical presuppositions have been smuggled in and portrayed as if they were scientifically verified facts.

Consider now the same paragraph, as rewritten by the Oxford systems biologist Denis Noble. Noble retains what is scientifically valid and verifiable in Dawkins's prose. Then, in a masterly piece of ideological subversion, he identifies *and inverts* Dawkins's nonscientific statements. Noble playfully portrays genes as passive, where Dawkins depicts them as active:

> [Genes] are trapped in huge colonies, locked inside highly intelligent beings, moulded by the outside world, communicating with it by complex processes, through which, blindly, as if by magic, function emerges. They are in you and me; we are the system that allows their code to be read; and their preservation is totally dependent on the joy that we experience in reproducing ourselves. We are the ultimate rationale for their existence.[17]

It will be clear that Dawkins and Noble represent the status of genes in completely different ways. The same limited scientific information is interpreted in totally different manners: in both cases, however, the metaphysical interpretation is being presented as scientific fact, on the same level as empirical statements. The point here is that both Dawkins and Noble cannot be right. Though both base themselves on the same observational statement, they import and impose quite different metaphysical assumptions upon it.

Their statements are thus "empirically equivalent," having equally good grounding in observation and experimental evidence. So which is right? How could we decide which is to be preferred on scientific grounds? As Noble observes, "no-one seems to be able to think of an experiment that would detect an empirical difference between them." The real problem with the way in which recent atheistic apologies use science as a weapon against religion has to do with the smuggling in of atheistic metaphysical assumptions, which the sciences themselves neither demand nor legitimize. As Noble's little piece of theatre shows us, some of what is presented as "science" by the New Atheism isn't really science at all: it actually amounts to the subversive manipulation of science by grafting on a patina of metaphysical naturalism.

So where does this leave us? The rhetoric of the New Atheism tries to characterize the movement as based on reason and science, dismissing all other alternatives—and especially religious alternatives—as outmoded irrational superstitions. This, however, is a position that can only be maintained by doing violence to both science and reason. The scientific method, when legitimately applied, simply does not take us to the destinations envisaged by the New Atheism. Science raises questions that it cannot answer, forcing us to ask deeper questions about this world and our place in it than the rather shallow rhetoric of recent populist atheism suggests.

So what happens if we try to trespass beyond the scientific horizon? What happens if we try to draw aside a curtain that was meant to stay closed? What lies beyond the scope of the scientific method?

Chapter 6

Beyond the Scientific Horizon

*I*n 1885, Thomas H. Huxley, the great champion of Charles Darwin's ideas in Victorian England, delivered a speech to mark the completion of a statue of Darwin, which would soon grace a London museum. In drawing the speech to a close, Huxley declares that science "commits suicide when it adopts a creed."[1] It is one of his most perceptive statements, and it deserves close attention.

Huxley is not simply noting the dangers which arise when science becomes the servant of the church or of any religious organization or theological orthodoxy. He sees equal danger in science's becoming the servant of a doctrinaire atheism, or being seen as a weapon in a war against religious belief. Science, he argues, is *science*, not a tool in the hands of those with aggressive religious or manipulative anti-religious agendas. Though often portrayed as a critic of religion, Huxley's main concern is to ensure that science is free to pursue its pursuit of truth without interference from dogmatism of any kind— whether religious or anti-religious.[2]

Science, when at its best and most authentic, has no creed, whether religious or anti-religious. As Huxley himself points out, it nevertheless has one, and only one, article of faith:

> The one act of faith in the convert to science, is the confession of the universality of order and of the absolute validity in all times and under all circumstances, of the law of causation. This confession is an act of faith, because, by the nature of the case, the truth of such propositions is not susceptible of proof.[3]

While there are those who insist that science makes and requires no judgement of faith, this is clearly not the case, in Huxley's view. Science finds itself dependent upon certain working beliefs which are not "susceptible of proof," which Huxley rightly terms "acts of faith."

For obvious reasons, New Atheist writers have been reluctant to draw attention to Huxley's insight, which contrasts sharply with the dogmatic insistence of Richard Dawkins that science is a faith-free zone. Dawkins is out of line with the philosophy of science here. Science has to make some basic assumptions—the sort of thing that the psychologist William James helpfully terms "working hypotheses." The astonishing, almost pathological aversion of the New Atheism to faith-based judgements in science ultimately seems to reflect little more than a prejudice against religion and its vocabulary. The philosopher of science Michael Polanyi is one of many writers to emphasize the fundamental importance of the scientific belief in the rationality of the natural world, along with an expectation that this will continue to manifest itself in the empirical investigation of the world.

Yet is science by itself capable of satisfying the human quest for meaning? One of the most perceptive discussions of this question comes from the pen of the Spanish philosopher José Ortega y Gasset (1883–1955), who celebrates science's capacity to explain our observations of the world, while nevertheless insisting on its failure to satisfy the deeper longings and questions of humanity. "Scientific truth is characterized by its exactness and the certainty of its predictions. But these admirable qualities are contrived by science at the cost of remaining on a plane of secondary problems, leaving intact the ultimate and decisive questions."[4] The fundamental virtue of science is that it knows when to stop. It only answers questions that it knows it can answer on the basis of the evidence. But human curiosity wants to go further than this. Human beings are unable "to do without all-around knowledge of the world, without an integral idea of the universe. Crude or refined, with our consent or without it, such a trans-scientific picture of the world will settle in the mind of each of us, ruling our lives more effectively than scientific truth."

Ortega y Gasset declares that the twentieth century witnessed unparalleled efforts to restrain humanity within the realm of the exact and determinable. A whole series of questions are needlessly and improperly declared to be "meaningless," because they go beyond the limits of the natural sciences. Ortega y Gasset declares that this premature dismissal extends to the great questions of life, such as "Where does the world come from, and whither is it going? Which is the supreme power of the cosmos, what the essential meaning of life?" However, we continue to wrestle with such ultimate questions of life, ignoring the demands of those who insist that they are meaningless. We cannot evade these questions, because wrestling with them is an inalienable aspect of being human. "We are given no escape from ultimate questions. In one way or another they are in us, whether we like it or not. Scientific truth is exact, but it is incomplete."

To be human is to yearn for meaning and answers to the riddles of existence. Yet the scientific enterprise stops short of those ultimate questions, and rightly so. It knows its limits, and its limits are determined by evidence. But sometimes that evidence seems to point beyond itself, to another world just over the horizon, beyond scientific investigation. Ortega y Gasset uses an illuminating image in making this point.

Science is but a small part of the human mind and organism. Where it stops, man does not stop. If the physicist detains[,] at the point where his method ends, the hand with which he delineates the facts, the human being behind each physicist prolongs the line thus begun and carries it on to its termination, as an eye beholding an arch in ruins will of itself complete the missing airy curve.

Ortega y Gasset's evocative image of the ruined arch enables us to grasp an important point. We are not talking about a blind leap of faith in the dark, but the continuation of an intellectual trajectory beyond the thresholds of the scientific method. Faith may go beyond reason and evidence; it does not go against them, but continues their lines of thought.

Since scientists are—and remain—human beings, Ortega y Gasset suggests that many scientists find themselves experiencing a tension between their scientific calling and their basic humanity. As scientists, they restrict themselves to the domain of the empirical and demonstrable; as human beings, they know the need to go beyond the empirical and speak about issues of meaning and value. The quest for the "good life" is just as important for scientists as it is for everyone else. Yet the scientist realizes that the natural sciences are not going to help us determine what is good. We noted earlier Richard Dawkins's observation that "science has no methods for deciding what is ethical."[5] I know of no scientist who dismisses ethical questions as meaningless or improper because science cannot answer them. Nor is the quest to lead the "good life" made redundant or delusional just because it involves going further than science can take us.

Science cannot deal with questions of meaning or value: it can only deal with matters of fact. Yet it is perfectly reasonable to ask whether deeper assumptions about the nature of reality—including the existence and nature and God—are embedded within the scientific method. Science makes no such explicit assumptions. But are such assumptions implicit? Does the scientific enterprise itself point to something which lies beyond its scope to investigate, yet upon which its successes ultimately depend? The theoretical chemist Charles A. Coulson, for example, points out the importance of religious convictions in explaining the "unprovable assumption that there is an order and constancy in Nature."[6] The British philosopher of religion Richard Swinburne takes this further, arguing that the explanatory capacity of faith in God is not limited to the fine details of reality, but extends beyond these to include the great questions of life that are either "too big" or "too odd" for science to explain.[7]

It is quite clear that many of the deepest and most engaging questions about the nature of the universe have their origins in a fundamentally religious quest for meaning. The concept of a lawful universe, with order that can be understood and trusted, emerged largely out of fundamental beliefs about the nature of God, expressed in the notion of the "laws of nature." Scientific advance has disclosed the fundamental explicability of much of the natural world. Though some might see this as eliminating any notion of mystery, others have rightly pointed out that it raises a far deeper question: Why can we explain things at all? Scientists are so used to being able to make sense of the world that they take it for granted.[8] Yet this is actually a rather curious phenomenon.

As Albert Einstein pointed out in 1936, "The eternal mystery of the world is its comprehensibility."[9] The fact that the world "is comprehensible is a miracle." For Einstein, explicability itself clearly requires explanation. The most incomprehensible thing about the universe is that it is comprehensible. The intelligibility of the natural world, demonstrated by the natural sciences, raises the fundamental question as to why there is such a fundamental resonance between the human mind and the structures of the universe. Here we see a general pattern: science raises questions which transcend its capacity to answer them. So where do we look for those answers?

All guides have their limits. Science is a good guide to truth, which falters when we yearn for meaning. If there is meaning within the world, science is simply not going to be able to disclose it. This is not a criticism of science. It is simply a plea to avoid discrediting science by making it say things that it can't defend by its own methods—such as whether there is a God.

So what of God? As the noted biologist Stephen Jay Gould and countless others have insisted, the question of the existence and nature of God lies beyond the scientific method.[10] It is certainly true that some aggressive atheists have tried to use science as a weapon against religion. Richard Dawkins, for example, argues that science and religion are locked in mortal combat today, just as they always have been. Scientists who believe in God are nothing more than collaborators or traitors, he claims.

Sadly, these views remain widespread in popular scientific culture. Yet as we noted earlier, historians of science have long since abandoned this "warfare" model of the relation of science and religion, as well as most of the alleged evidence in its support,[11] pointing out that the relationship is far more complex than this simplistic stereotype suggests. Yet this historically outdated and scholarly debunked notion seems to be integral to Dawkins's defence of his atheism in *The God Delusion* and elsewhere. The God whom Dawkins rejects is substantially derived from media stereotypes and urban myths, and his understanding of the relationship between science and theology seems to originate from the writings of Andrew Dickson White (1832–1918), most notably his *History of the Warfare of Science with Theology* (1896), whose shallow scholarship has been soundly rubbished by historians of science.

Dawkins also argues that science explains (or has the potential to explain) everything, including matters traditionally regarded as lying within the religious realm. The traditional scientific positivist outlook that seems so characteristic of the New Atheism holds that science and religion offer competing explanations. One day science will triumph, and religious explanations will fade away. There cannot be multiple explanations of the same things, and only the scientific explanation can be valid, claims the New Atheism.

Yet this is actually a very nineteenth-century way of arguing, resting on a failure to think critically about the nature of scientific explanation. Neuroscientist Max Bennett and philosopher Peter Hacker have recently explored the science-explains-everything outlook that Dawkins and others espouse: they have found it seriously wanting.[12] For example, scientific theories cannot be said to "explain the world"—only to explain the *phenomena* which are observed within the world. Furthermore, Bennett and Hacker argue, scientific theories do not, and are not intended to, describe and explain "everything about the world," such as its purpose. Law, economics, and sociology are examples of disciplines which engage with domain-specific phenomena, without in any way having to regard themselves as somehow being inferior to the natural sciences or dependent upon them.

The real issue has to do with levels of explanation. We live in a complex, multi-layered universe. Each level has to be included in our analysis. Physics, chemistry, biology, and psychology—to note only four sciences—engage with different levels of reality and offer explanations appropriate to that level. But they are not individually exhaustive. A comprehensive explanation must bring together these different levels of explanation, in that (to give an obvious example) the physical explanation of an electron is not in competition with its chemical counterpart.

My Oxford colleague John Lennox, who is a mathematician and philosopher of science, uses a neat illustration to make this point. Imagine a cake being subjected to scientific analysis, leading to an exhaustive discussion of its chemical composition and of the physical forces which hold it together. Does this tell us that the cake was baked to celebrate a birthday? And is this inconsistent with the scientific analysis? Of course not. Science and theology ask different questions: in the case of science, the question concerns how things happen: by what process? In the case of theology, the question is why things happen: to what purpose?

Imagine a cake being subjected to scientific analysis, leading to an exhaustive discussion of its chemical composition and of the physical forces which hold it together. Does this tell us that the cake was baked to celebrate a birthday? And is this inconsistent with the scientific analysis? Of course not. Science and theology ask different questions.

Here we see the important scientific principle of different levels of explanation, which supplement each other. This principle can easily be explored from everyday life. Consider a performance of your favourite piece of music. This can be scientifically described in terms of patterns of vibrations. Yet this perfectly valid explanation requires supplementation if it is to account for the full significance of the phenomenon of music and its impact upon us. Similarly, there is far more to a great painting than an analysis of its chemical components or the physical arrangement of its elements. Scientific and religious explanations can thus supplement each other. The problems start when scientists start pretending to be religious or theologians start pretending to be scientists. Science tells us a story about the history and nature of the world which we know and inhabit. But it does not tell the full story. Christianity is consistent with the story told by science, but it takes that story further. It tells the full story, of which science is but part.

At a very simple level, we could apply this approach like this. A scientific description of the world accounts for how it arose from an initial cosmological event (the fiery singularity of the "big bang"), which led, over a long period of time, to the formation of stars and planets, creating conditions favourable to the origination and evolution of living creatures. No reference is made or needs to be made to God. The Christian will speak of God bringing the world into existence and directing it towards its intended outcomes. For some, this process involves direct divine action; for others, it involves God's creating and working through natural forces to achieve those goals. Yet these supplement each other's accounts rather than contradicting each other.

A further argument advanced by Dawkins is that belief in God can be explained away on scientific grounds. One of Dawkins's most characteristic and influential beliefs, which is repeated in the leading works of the New Atheism, is that belief in God is a delusion caused by "memes." Dawkins first introduced the idea of the meme back in 1976. Towards the end of his *Selfish Gene*, he argues that there is a basic analogy between biological and cultural evolution: both involve a replicator. In the case of biological evolution, this replicator is the gene; in the case of cultural evolution, it is a hypothesized entity, which Dawkins called a "meme."

For Dawkins, the idea of God is perhaps the supreme example of such a meme. People do not believe in God because they have given long and careful thought to the matter: they do so because they have been infected by a powerful meme, which has somehow "leapt" into their brains. Clearly the psychology of this approach is deeply problematic. Human minds don't just passively absorb or generate ideas. Dawkins seems to think that we develop ideas in much the same way as we develop flu—we become infected by someone else.

In *The God Delusion* (2006), Dawkins sets out the idea of memes as if it were established scientific orthodoxy, making no mention of the inconvenient fact that it has been relegated to the margins of mainstream scientific thought.[13] Dawkins presents the "meme" as if it were an actually existing entity, with huge potential to explain the origins of religion. Dawkins is even able to develop an advanced vocabulary based on his own convictions—such as "memeplex." Daniel Dennett also makes extensive use of the idea in his New Atheist manifesto *Breaking the Spell* (2006). The intellectual case for New Atheism has come to depend heavily on the idea of the meme, yet the serious problems with this notion have decidedly awkward consequences for this supposedly "scientific" approach to atheism.

To illustrate some of the difficulties of this approach, we may consider Dawkins's characteristically bold and confident statement that "memes can sometimes display very high fidelity."[14] On the surface, this appears to be a statement of scientific fact. Yet on closer examination, it is nothing of the sort. Dawkins is actually restating an observation into his own idiosyncratic theoretical framework. The *observation* is the uncontestable and uncontroversial fact that ideas can be passed from one individual, group, or generation to another; Dawkins's controversial *theoretical interpretation* of this observation—which is here presented as if it were fact—involves attributing fidelity to what most regard as being a non-existent entity. This is perhaps the greatest failing of memetics: its "achievements" are

limited to simply *redescribing* a range of phenomena in its own idiosyncratic terms.

Furthermore, neither ideas nor cultural artefacts can be said either
to be, or to contain, a self-assembly code. They are not "replicators,"
as required by the accounts of cultural transmission and development
offered by Dawkins and Dennett.[15] Indeed, since there is no compelling scientific evidence for these entities, some have playfully—
though not without good reason—concluded that there might even
be a meme for believing in memes. To its many critics, the meme is
just a biological fiction.

One telling indication of the failure of the meme theory to garner
academic support can be seen in the history of the online *Journal of
Memetics*, launched in 1997, arguably at the zenith of the cultural
plausibility of the meme.[16] The journal ceased publication in 2005.
Why? The answer can be found in a devastating critique of the notion
of the meme, published in the final issue of this journal, in which Dr
Bruce Edmonds makes two fundamental criticisms of the notion of
memes, which he believes have undermined its claims to plausibility
in the scientific community.[17]

1. Memetics has fundamentally failed because it "has not provided
any extra explanatory or predictive power beyond that available
without the gene-meme analogy." In other words, it has not provided
any added value and new insights in terms of providing a genuinely
new understanding of phenomena.

2. Memetics has been characterized by "theoretical discussion
of extreme abstraction and over-ambition." Edmonds singles out
for special criticism unrealistic and over-ambitious attempts, often
developed in advance of evidence, "to 'explain' some immensely
complex phenomena such as religion." Yet for many of its more
fanatical advocates, this is precisely the point of memetics: to explain
away belief in God.

Edmonds ends his incisive dismissal of the meme with what has
turned out to be its epitaph: Memetics, Edmonds suggests, "has been
a short-lived fad whose effect has been to obscure more than it has
been to enlighten. I am afraid that memetics, as an identifiable disci-
pline, will not be widely missed."

The importance of this observation will be obvious. As we noted
earlier, two of the leading works of the New Atheism make an appeal

to the meme an integral part of their scientific case for arguing that belief in God can be explained away (most scientists would prefer to say "reductively explained"). Yet the notion of the meme turns out to be highly speculative, and it is significantly under-determined by the evidence. It remains to be seen what the long-term implications of this excessive reliance on such "a short-lived fad" (as termed by Edmonds) will be for atheist apologetics.

The idea that science "disproves" God is the kind of immensely simplistic statement that has featured prominently in recent populist atheism. It makes atheists feel good and encourages them to believe that the entire scientific enterprise is supportive of their beliefs. But it's simply not right. It may be slick and simple, but it doesn't square up with the way things are. Dawkins is simply wrong in asserting that all real scientists are or ought to be atheists. Why are so many scientists religious, despite the professional criticism that their faith often attracts?

The obvious and most intellectually satisfying explanation of this is not difficult to identify. It is well known that the natural world is conceptually malleable. It can be interpreted, without any loss of intellectual integrity, in a number of different ways. Some "read" or "interpret" nature in an atheistic way. Others "read" it in a deistic way, seeing it as pointing to a creator divinity, who is no longer involved in its affairs. God winds up the clock and then leaves it to work on its own. Others take a more specifically Christian view, believing in a God who both creates and sustains. Others take a more spiritualized view, speaking more vaguely of some "life force."

The point is simple: nature is open to many legitimate interpretations. Science, in itself and of itself, is neutral. It can be interpreted in atheist, deist, theist, and many other ways—but it does not demand to be interpreted in any of these ways. One can be a real scientist without being committed to any specific religious, spiritual, or anti-religious view of the world. This, I may add, is the view of most scientists I speak to, including those who self-define as atheists. Unlike Dawkins, they can understand perfectly well why some of their colleagues adopt a Christian view of the world. They may not agree with that approach, but they're prepared to respect it.

Yet this leaves open the question that we have explored in earlier chapters. Since nature can be interpreted in many ways, which is the best interpretation? Since the universe can be explained in different manners, which is the *best* of these explanations? How well does any given framework of meaning make sense of what is actually observed? Earlier, we noted C. S. Lewis's characteristic assertion that Christianity makes sense in itself and makes sense of everything else. So what is this lens that the Christian brings to the observation of the world? What are its key elements? In the following chapter, we shall consider some of the basic themes of the Christian way of making sense of the world.

Chapter 7

A Christian Viewpoint

"*I* believe in Christianity as I believe that the Sun has risen, not only because I see it, but because by it, I see everything else" (C. S. Lewis).[1] These carefully crafted words express Lewis's core belief in the rationality of the Christian faith. Lewis (1898–1963) came to believe in God partly through his deepening conviction that God was to be compared to an intellectual sun which illuminated the landscape of reality. The Christian faith was, for Lewis, like a lens which allowed things to be seen in sharp focus. Its capacity to illuminate and make sense of reality was, he argued, an indication (but not a proof) of its truth. Not every enigma was resolved; for Lewis, the question of suffering would remain a major cause of intellectual discomfort, particularly in later life.[2] Yet his faith in God offered him an Archimedean point from which he could make sense of the riddles and puzzles of the world.

In speaking of believing in Christianity as being analogous to believing that the sun has risen, Lewis makes two quite different, though related, points. First, it makes sense to believe in God. Head and heart, reason and imagination—all point us towards their goal in God. They may not take us all the way to faith, but they point us in the right direction. Second, Lewis argues that belief in God gives us a way of framing the world, allowing it to be seen properly. Faith in God is the lens that brings reality into sharp focus, the sun that lights up the world so that it may be seen more fully and clearly. Belief in God makes sense in itself and makes sense of everything else—including the success and limits of the natural sciences.

49

Yet an objection might be raised here. Christians talk about salvation rather than explanation. They speak about worshipping God or praying to God, rather than thinking of God as some sort of cosmic reference handbook. The idea of God making sense of things seems to play a smaller role in everyday Christian thinking than Lewis appears to suggest. Earlier we noted Terry Eagleton's incisive statement that "Christianity was never meant to be an explanation of anything in the first place."

It is true that there is more to Christianity than trying to make sense of things. The gospel is not so much about explanation as about salvation: the transformation of human existence through the life, death, and resurrection of Jesus of Nazareth. Nevertheless, though the emphasis of the Christian proclamation may not be on explaining the world, it also offers a distinctive way of looking at things which, at least in principle, enables us to see things in different ways and thus leads us to act in ways consistent with this. Christianity involves believing that certain things are true, that they may be relied upon, and that they illuminate our perceptions, decisions, and actions.

The New Testament uses a wide range of images to describe this transformation, many of which suggest a change in the way in which we see things. It speaks of our eyes being opened, and a veil being removed (Acts 9:9–19; 2 Cor. 3:13–16). Throughout his letters, we find Paul reaffirming the transformative power of the gospel, emphasizing its capacity to change human lives, including the way in which we understand the world and behave within it and towards it.[3] "Do not be conformed to this world, but be transformed by the renewing of your minds" (Rom. 12:2). Although the Christian emphasis is on transformation of the human situation, not on how we explain things, part of the rich tapestry of faith concerns how the gospel's "renewal of the mind" leads to new ways of understanding the world. We see it in new ways and so come to understand it in new terms.

Lewis's argument is that Christianity provides a framework, a way of thinking, which makes more sense of the world than its alternatives, including his own former atheism. To put this somewhat formally: Christianity is characterized at one and the same time by its intra-systemic elegance and its extra-systemic fecundity. The Christian vision of reality possesses an internal coherence and consistency which is at least matched by its remarkable ability to make sense of what we observe and experience. Christian theology has a conceptual spaciousness which allows it to accommodate the natural sciences, art, morality, and other religious traditions. Christianity has the capacity to make sense of the world, simultaneously reinforcing the intellectual case for the existence of God while offering a way of "seeing nature" that enables us to appreciate and respect it in ways that would otherwise not be possible.

Seeing nature—we must linger momentarily on that highly significant phrase. Lewis declares that the Christian faith allows us to see things *as they really are*. Yet we are unable to see things as they actually are unless we are helped to see them properly. The British moral philosopher and novelist Iris Murdoch (1919–99) pointed out that "by opening our eyes we do not necessarily see what confronts us. . . . Our minds are continually active, fabricating an anxious, usually self-preoccupied, often falsifying *veil* which partially conceals the world."[4] This veil needs to be removed so that we can see properly. The gospel allows this veil to be drawn aside so that we can see things clearly for what they really are.

This point was made repeatedly by the great English cultural critic and commentator John Ruskin (1819–1900), who declares that "the greatest thing a human soul ever does in this world is to see something, and tell what it saw in a plain way. . . . To see clearly is poetry, prophecy, and religion—all in one."[5] Ruskin here put his finger on what many theologians of his age overlooked—that the Christian mind does not passively receive impressions of nature but actively interprets it. The process of observation, whether scientific or religious, involves trying to match what is observed with what is believed and then making any necessary adjustments.

Furthermore, we must learn to see nature *as a whole*. One of the more unsatisfactory aspects of some traditional "proofs" for the existence of God is their tendency to seek explanatory gaps within nature and then try to plug them through an appeal to special or covert divine presence or activity. Whatever science could not currently explain, or more exactly, whatever one could make a case for holding that science could never in principle explain, was to be deemed the "special" work of God. Yet the approach to natural theology that I believe arises from within the Christian tradition involves seeing nature as a totality, seeking the explanatory "big picture." How do we account for our capacity to explain things so well? How do we account for the "unreasonable effectiveness of mathematics,"[6] the creation of the human mind that seems to be sculpted precisely to the contours of the universe?

The so-called God-of-the-Gaps approach tries to defend the existence of God by an appeal to gaps in scientific explanation. I must confess that I have never been impressed by this approach. While studying chemistry as an undergraduate at Oxford University back in the early 1970s, I came to know and respect Charles Coulson (1910–74), Oxford University's first professor of theoretical chemistry, who was a vigorous critic of this approach. For Coulson, reality as a whole demanded explanation: "Either God is in the whole of Nature, with no gaps, or He's not there at all."[7] Much the same point was made earlier by the Scottish theologian Henry Drummond (1851–97):

> How do we account for our capacity to explain things so well? How do we account for the "unreasonable effectiveness of mathematics," the creation of the human mind that seems to be sculpted precisely to the contours of the universe?

When things are known, that is to say, we conceive them as natural, on Man's level; when they are unknown, we call them divine—as if our ignorance of a thing were the stamp of its divinity. If God is only to be left to the gaps in our knowledge, where shall we be when these gaps are filled up? And if they are never to be filled up, is God only to be found in the disorders of the world? Those who yield to the temptation to reserve a point here and there for special divine interposition are apt to forget that this virtually excludes God from the rest of the process.[8]

Christianity is not seen at its best if it becomes preoccupied with looking for temporary explanatory gaps in the scientific view of the world. God is not to be found in the gaps and recesses of the world. God is the one who gives meaning to the whole universe, who alone is able to explain why there is anything at all and to explain what it means. The Christian faith offers an alternative way of viewing nature, which at times may challenge exaggerated versions of the scientific method; yet it welcomes and sees itself as part of the human quest for truth, whether scientific or religious. Christian faith, when subjected to the same rational scrutiny that science demands of its data and theories, shows an honest pursuit of truth accompanied by a confidence in its rational motivation. It expects to find, and does in fact find, a significant explanatory resonance with what is known of nature from other sources, while at the same time insisting on its own right to depict and describe nature in its own special way—as God's creation.

So what way of "seeing" reality does Christianity make possible? We need to make it clear that the rich vision of God which excites and informs the Christian faith goes far beyond the somewhat impersonal notions of God that are often found in traditional defences of the existence of God—such as the remote and detached idea of a creator God, often dubbed "the divine watchmaker." Rather, reality is seen in the light of the glorious Christian vision of God as Father, Son, and Spirit: a God who creates, redeems, and sanctifies; a God who is present with us at this moment, while remaining the transcendent ground of order and existence within the universe. This vision of God moves us to worship and prayer, where the older vision of God as the watchmaker leads at most to admiration of technical competency.

The process of reflection on reality that has its origins from within the Christian faith is guided and nourished by this vision of God. The grand themes of the Christian faith provide an interpretative framework by which nature may be seen, allowing it to be viewed and read in profound and significant ways. Christian theology is the elixir, the philosopher's stone, which turns the mundane into the epiphanic, the world of nature into the realm of God's creation.

Like a lens bringing a vast landscape into sharp focus, or a map helping us grasp the features of the terrain around us, Christian doctrine offers a new way of understanding, imagining, and behaving. It invites us to see the natural order, and our selves within it, in a special way—a way that might be hinted at, but cannot be confirmed by, the natural order itself. Nature is "seen" as God's creation; the "book of nature" is read as God's story—and ours. It is as if a veil has been lifted, or a bright sun has illuminated a mental landscape.

So how does this impact how we see nature? How good is this framework at making sense of what we observe? Limits on space mean that I must restrict myself to exploring just two of its many aspects. We shall consider, briefly, the notion of the "economy of salvation" and the idea that humanity bears the image of God. Each of these are integral elements of the Christian vision of reality; each casts light on reality, illuminating its complex landscape and allowing us to understand what we see.

We begin by considering the concept of the "economy of salvation," which sets out the idea that God's interaction with the world is described in terms of a narrative of creation, fall, redemption, and final consummation. The notion of the economy of salvation, although clearly developed in the New Testament, was given its traditional formulation by the second-century writer Irenaeus of Lyons.[9] Reacting against gnostic interpretations of salvation history in the late second century, Irenaeus laid out a panoramic vision of the economy of salvation, insisting that the entire breadth of history, from creation to consummation, was the work of one and the same triune God. Both the human observer and the natural things observed are located in "the midst of this era" (Augustine of Hippo)—in other words, at a point that is theologically distant and removed from the creation that was declared to be "good" in the creation narrative. That creation now groans, and those groanings are observed by those whose judgements are clouded and obscured by sin. This leads to the theologically significant conclusion that a fallen humanity reflects on a fallen world of nature.

Hints of the importance of this consideration can be seen within the New Testament. For example, it is well known that Paul makes an appeal to creation as the basis of a knowledge of God. Yet while Paul clearly holds that God can be known through the creation (Rom. 1), at other points he qualifies this by referring to the "groaning" of the creation (Rom. 8). The created order is to be seen as in transition, from what it once was to what it finally will become. There is a profoundly eschatological dimension to an authentically Christian natural theology, in that the natural order should be observed in the light of its goal, not merely in the light of its origination. Paul's statements can thus not only be interpreted in terms of the fall of creation from its original state, but also as an extension of the Old Testament prophetic theme of the hope for the future renewal and restoration of creation.

The importance of this point is easily appreciated when we consider this question: Why is there evil in the world? Why is there suffering in a supposedly good creation? The Christian framework of the economy of salvation helps us to appreciate that we have to locate this problem on a theological map. The world was created good; one day it will be restored to an even greater goodness. The images of the garden of Eden and the new Jerusalem are visual markers for key moments of this narrative. At present, we are located within this journey, not at its beginning or end. This idea of journeying within the context of the economy of salvation was often expressed in the Middle Ages by using the Latin term *viator* (wayfarer/traveller).

The theological framework set out in the economy of salvation affirms that God has created all things good and that they will finally be restored to goodness. Yet at the present, it insists that good and evil coexist in the world, as wheat and weeds grow together in the same field (Matt. 13:24–30). Without collapsing one into the other, it allows us to locate good and evil within the context of the theological trajectory of creation, fall, incarnation, redemption, and consummation.

Our second theme is that God created humanity bearing the "image of God" (Gen. 1:27). This is widely interpreted by Christian theologians as affirming two central themes: first, that humanity is able to relate to God in a manner analogous to other personal relationships; and second, that humanity has been created with the capacity to make sense of God's creation. The fourth-century theologian Athanasius summarizes this second point as follows: Humanity was created by God in such a way that, "by looking into the heights of heaven, and perceiving the harmony of creation, they might know its ruler, the Word of the Father, who, by his own providence over all things, makes the Father known to all."[10] Although Athanasius holds that human nature has been corrupted by sin, he still maintains that humanity retains a God-given capacity to discern its creator within the created order.

This point is of obvious importance in dealing with one of the most discussed features of the universe: its intelligibility. Scientific advance has disclosed the fundamental explicability of much of the natural world. Though some might see this as eliminating any notion of mystery, others have rightly pointed out that it raises a far deeper question: Why can we explain things at all? We have already noted

Albert Einstein's emphatic assertion that "the eternal mystery of the world is its comprehensibility." For Einstein, explicability itself clearly requires explanation. The most incomprehensible thing about the universe is that it is comprehensible. The *intelligibility* of the natural world, demonstrated by the natural sciences, raises the fundamental question as to why there is such a fundamental resonance between human minds and the structures of the universe. From a Trinitarian perspective, this resonance between the human mind and the deep structure of the universe is to be explained by the rationality of God as creator of the fundamental ordering of nature and of the human observer of nature.

The theologian and physicist John Polkinghorne (born in 1930) is one of many who have grasped the importance of this point. Polkinghorne points out that "modern science seems, almost irresistibly, to point beyond itself." A scientifically disclosed universe that is ordered and intelligible clearly needs explanation, unless we are to suggest that our capacity to make sense of the universe is simply accidental or random:

> We are so familiar with the fact that we can understand the world that most of the time we take it for granted. It is what makes science possible. Yet it could have been otherwise. The universe might have been a disorderly chaos rather than an orderly cosmos. Or it might have had a rationality which was inaccessible to us. . . . There is a congruence between our minds and the universe, between the rationality experienced within and the rationality observed without.[11]

There is a clear need, Polkinghorne argues, for "an intellectually satisfying understanding of what would otherwise be unintelligible good fortune." Both the scientist and the theologian thus work by faith, a trust in the rational reliability of our understanding of experience.

Earlier we emphasized the importance of the laws of nature. But where do these laws of physics actually come from? Why are they the way they are? And why can they be represented so well by mathematics? A typical atheist's answer is that there is no reason at all why the laws of physics take their present form. That's just the way things are, and there is no need to explain anything. These laws of nature exist without any reason and without any need for a reason.

Yet if this is the case, then the universe could be argued to be ultimately absurd, since no reason may be given for either its present laws or its present forms. This leads to a troubling conclusion that the entire scientific enterprise—which is ultimately grounded on the notion that there are natural reasons for physical phenomena and that such explanations are rational and logical—is ultimately rooted in absurdity or an accident. If that is so, we must ask why such an absurd universe seems to mimic the rational universe of the mathematicians. Perhaps it is purely accidental, a piece of good fortune for mathematicians and cosmologists alike. But it's not a particularly persuasive answer.

The argument of this book is that Christianity offers an intellectual sun that illuminates an otherwise dark and enigmatic world: it gives a deeply satisfying "empirical fit" between theory and observation, which suggests that the map of reality that it offers is reliable and may be trusted. In what follows, we shall explore how it makes sense of some aspects of the world.

We begin by reflecting on what we know about the beginning of the universe.

Chapter 8

The Deep Structure of the Universe

As we saw earlier, current thinking about the origins of the universe points to a primordial big bang, leading to the gradual emergence of the universe as we now know it.[1] Yet the evolution of the universe is shaped by the fundamental constants of nature. Close examination of the cosmic narrative just outlined suggests that its shape and outcome was determined by some critically important factors. It is clear that there exist certain invariant properties of the natural world and its elementary components which make the gross size and structure of almost all its composite objects inevitable. The size of bodies such as stars and planets are neither random nor the result of any progressive selection process, but simply manifestations of the different strengths of the various forces of nature. If these were different, the universe would have taken a very different form. Human beings might not have been here. For the Christian, the universe is a creation that has been endowed by its creator with precisely those laws of nature that are necessary for it to have so fruitful a history, leading to the appearance of humanity.

Since the seventeenth century, it had been widely assumed that no special initial conditions were required for the emergence of a life-bearing universe.[2] Yet in the last few decades, it has become clear that this is not the case. There has been a growing realization of the extraordinary degree of contingency of the initial conditions of the universe, if heavy elements, planets, and ultimately complex life were to develop. The life-bearing properties of the universe are highly sensitive to the values of the fundamental forces and con-

58

stants of nature. The theoretical physicist Lee Smolin points to the importance of this point in relation to the development of stars:

> The existence of stars rests on several delicate balances between the different forces in nature. These require that the parameters that govern how strongly these forces act be tuned just so. In many cases, a small turn of the dial in one direction or another results in a world not only without stars, but [also] with much less structure than our universe.[3]

A life-bearing universe is far more constrained than had been realized. This has led many to speak of the universe being "fine-tuned" for life. The deep structure of the universe seems to have been designed to allow life to come into existence.[4]

The term "fine-tuning" is often used to refer to the scientific realization that the values of certain fundamental cosmological constants and the character of certain initial conditions of the universe appear to have played a decisive role in bringing about the emergence of a particular kind of universe, within which intelligent life can develop. Many recent scientific studies have emphasized the significance of certain fundamental cosmological constants which, if varied slightly, would have significant implications for the emergence of human existence.[5] Examples of the astrophysical "fine-tuning" of fundamental cosmological constants include the following:

1. If the strong coupling constant were slightly smaller, hydrogen would be the only element in the universe. Since the evolution of life as we know it is fundamentally dependent on the chemical properties of carbon, that life could not have come into being without some hydrogen being converted to carbon by fusion. On the other hand, if the strong coupling constant were slightly larger (even by as much as 2 percent), the hydrogen would have been converted to helium, with the result that no long-lived stars would have been formed. Since such stars are regarded as essential to the emergence of life, such a conversion would have led to life as we know it failing to emerge.

2. If the weak fine constant were slightly smaller, no hydrogen would have formed during the early history of the universe. Consequently, no stars would have been formed. On the other hand, if it were slightly larger, supernovae would have been unable to eject the

heavier elements necessary for life. In either case, life as we know it could not have emerged.

3. If the electromagnetic fine structure constant were slightly larger, the stars would not be hot enough to warm planets to a temperature sufficient to maintain life in the form in which we know it. If smaller, the stars would have burned out too quickly to allow life to evolve on these planets.

4. If the gravitational fine structure constant were slightly smaller, stars and planets would not have been able to form because they would have lacked the gravitational constraints necessary for coalescence of their constituent material. If stronger, the stars thus formed would have burned out too quickly to allow the evolution of life.

The important point to appreciate is that each of these four statements is framed *counterfactually*. We are asked to envisage alternative worlds in which these constants have different values, and then to compare these worlds with that which we actually know. Small variations in any of these constants would have led to very different outcomes. For a theist, the implications of such points are obvious: as the philosopher John Leslie shrewdly observes, "God would need to be careful which physics he chose."[6]

We could imagine a mental experiment in which someone designs a machine that allows us to vary the values of some of the fundamental properties of the universe—such as the weak nuclear force—and see what would happen (at least theoretically) if they were significantly different from what is actually observed. The surprisingly restricted range of values that certain fundamental constants must take to bring about the universe with which we are familiar has led the physicist Paul Davies and others to speak of God as the cosmic "fine-tuner."

> Life as we know it depends very sensitively on the form of the laws of physics, and on some seemingly fortuitous accidents in the actual values that nature has chosen for various particle masses, force strengths, and so on. If we could play God, and select values for these natural quantities at whim by twiddling a set of knobs, we would find that almost all knob settings would render the universe uninhabitable. Some knobs would have to be fine-tuned to enormous precision if life is to flourish in the universe.[7]

Some landmarks in the development of the notion of "fine-tuning" should be noted. In 1973, Barry Collins and Steven Hawking pointed out that, out of all the possible values of the physical constants, only a relatively narrow range of initial conditions could give rise to the observed isotropy of the actual universe.[8] A quite extraordinary degree of constraint would have to be imposed on the initial cosmic energy density to give rise to the universe as we know it. They found this result puzzling: accepted theories did not offer any explanation for the fact that the universe turned out this way rather than another. Collins and Hawking argue that a universe beginning with too much gravitational energy would re-collapse before it could form stars, and a universe with too little energy would not permit the gravitational condensation of galaxies and stars. Thus, out of many different possible initial values of Ω (the ratio of the actual average density of the universe to the critical density), human life could only have emerged in a universe where the initial value of Ω was almost precisely 1.

A year later, Brandon Carter published a paper in which he introduced the term "the anthropic principle," which he stated in two forms. The *weak* anthropic principle holds that "what we can expect to observe must be restricted by the conditions necessary for our presence as observers." The *strong* anthropic principle holds that "the universe (and hence the fundamental parameters on which it depends) must be such as to admit the creation of observers within it at some stage."[9]

These speculative explorations culminated in 1986 with the publication of John Barrow and Frank Tipler's landmark book, *The Anthropic Cosmological Principle*, which propelled the "anthropic principle" from the pages of obscure journals to popular culture.[10] In doing so, it has raised many theological questions, including the apologetic value of the "anthropic principle." Barrow and Tipler provide a comprehensive yet relatively accessible account of the fundamental role played by the constants of nature, and the astonishing great implications of seemingly small variations in their magnitude. *The Anthropic Cosmological Principle* set out the extraordinary, seemingly fortuitous coincidences that appear to have made life possible. Barrow and Tipler go on to present three possible ways of making sense of apparent "fine-tuning" of the world for biological life: the "weak," "strong," and "final" forms of the principle. Although each of these models was already known within the scientific community, Barrow and Tipler made them intelligible and accessible to a much wider readership. It rapidly became the "Bible of anthropic reasoning" (according to Robert Klee).

Barrow and Tipler challenge the popular secular myth that talk about "design" of the world is a recent innovation. As they rightly point out, it is one of the oldest and most fundamental questions of all, deriving its legitimacy partly from its antiquity and partly from its sheer intellectual importance. "Aristotelian science was based upon presupposition of an intelligent natural world that functions according to some deliberate design." The English popular religious writer William Paley (1743–1805) developed the "argument from design" in some new directions in the early nineteenth century.[11] This approach is now regarded as unsatisfactory. Yet Paley's intellectual and theological misadventures, which are clearly specific to this age, cannot be allowed to negate the question of why things are the way they are—or indeed, why there is anything at all.

Barrow addresses such issues in subsequent writings, making the fair point that two quite different forms of the design argument are used by theologians and philosophers. The first is that which is encountered in the larger, biological, section of Paley's *Natural Theology*, and it is based on "nice outcomes of the laws of nature." The argument, though easily grasped, is severely vulnerable. God can easily be eliminated from the argument (a development which began long before Darwin published his theory of natural selection). In my view, it amounts to little more than deism, positing a somewhat attenuated notion of God rather than the somewhat richer Trinitarian vision of God associated with Christianity.

Barrow's second approach is based on "nice laws." Where do the laws of nature come from? If the universe sprang into existence in an astonishingly short time *already possessing the laws that would govern its development*, the question of the origin and character of those laws becomes of major apologetic importance. As Barrow rightly points out, this latter version of the design argument is much harder to explain without reference to God. After all, the laws of nature clearly did not come into being by a gradual process of cumulative selection. The universe that emerged out of the big bang, on an anthropic reading of things, was already governed by laws that were fine-tuned to encourage the rise of carbon-based life forms.

The apparent fine-tuning of the universe has been considered in a large number of relatively accessible recent works.[12] For our purposes, it is enough to note several features that illustrate this phenomenon rather than provide a more extended analysis. The debate in the literature mainly concerns the *interpretation* of these phenomena, whose existence is generally conceded. The essential point is that if the values of certain fundamental constants which govern the development of the universe had been slightly different, its evolution would have taken a different course, leading to a cosmos in which life would not have been possible. The element of surprise in this analysis relates to the impact on cosmic evolution of even a small variation of some of these constants.

For a recent statement regarding the importance of the fine balancing of the universe's fundamental constants, we may turn to Sir Martin Rees, currently president of the Royal Society of London, Britain's leading association of scientists.[13] We may summarize his analysis of these constants as follows:

1. *The ratio of the electromagnetic force to the force of gravity*, which can also be expressed in terms of the electrical (coulomb) force between two protons divided by the gravitational force between them. This measures the strength of the electrical forces that hold atoms together, divided by the force of gravity between them. If this were slightly smaller than its observed value, "only a short-lived miniature universe could exist: no creatures could grow larger than insects, and there would be no time for biological evolution."

2. *The strong nuclear force*, which defines how firmly atomic nuclei bind together. This force "controls the power from the Sun and, more sensitively, how stars transmute hydrogen into all the atoms of the periodic table." Once more, the value of this constant turns out to

be of critical importance. Even a small variation in its value would lead to the development of a universe in which we would not exist.

3. *The amount of matter in the universe.* The cosmic number Ω (omega) is a measure of the amount of material in our universe—such as galaxies, diffuse gas, and so-called dark matter and dark energy. Ω tells us the relative importance of gravity and expansion energy in the universe. "If this ratio were too high relative to a particular 'critical' value, the universe would have collapsed long ago; had it been too low, no galaxies or stars would have formed. The initial expansion speed seems to have been finely tuned."

4. *Cosmic repulsion.* In 1998, cosmologists became aware of the importance of cosmic antigravity in controlling the expansion of the universe, and in particular its increasing importance as our universe becomes ever darker and emptier. "Fortunately for us (and very surprisingly to theorists), λ is very small. Otherwise its effect would have stopped galaxies and stars from forming, and cosmic evolution would have been stifled before it could even begin."

5. *The ratio of the gravitational binding force to rest-mass energy,* Q, is of fundamental importance in determining the "texture" of the universe. "If Q were smaller, the universe would be inert and structureless; if Q were much larger, it would be a violent place, in which no stars or solar systems could survive, dominated by vast black holes."

6. *The number of spatial dimensions,* D, which is three. String theory argues that, of the ten or eleven original dimensions at the origins of the universe, all but three were compactified. Time, of course, is to be treated as a fourth dimension. "Life," Rees comments, "couldn't exist if D were two or four."

These six points can easily be expanded to include a series of observations about the values of fundamental constants, or the initial boundary conditions of the universe. As Freeman Dyson once remarked, "The more I examine the universe and study the details of its architecture, the more evidence I find that the universe in some sense must have known that we were coming."

So how are we to assess these new developments in cosmology, which are clearly of considerable theological significance? Though there are dissenting voices, it is widely agreed that the "new cosmology" is consonant with theism. Some would go further and argue that the phenomenon of fine-tuning gives new life to more rigorous forms of inductive or deductive argumentation for the existence of God, such as the teleological and cosmological arguments. The realization that the universe as a whole, and not simply life on earth, has a history has major implications for our understanding of the emergence of life, often ignored in biological works. For example, many accounts of biological evolution often seem to assume that it is utterly unproblematic, and perhaps even uninteresting, that the critical chemical materials required for life are present in the universe, with physical properties that facilitate both the emergence and development of living forms.

Thus the issue of fine-tuning is no longer being limited to a discussion of cosmology. Since about 1990, there has been growing awareness that other scientific disciplines are generating material that is open to a similar interpretation. In particular, there has been a growing realization of the interconnections between certain fundamental principles of biology and astrophysics. In the following chapter, we shall consider these developments before moving on to reflect more fully on their significance.

Chapter 9

The Mystery of the Possibility of Life

*O*ne of the most significant scientific discoveries of the last generation is that the universe was pregnant with the possibility of human
existence right from its very start. The laws of nature seem to be
"fine-tuned" in order to make life possible. As we noted in an earlier chapter, the early universe produced nearly nothing other than
hydrogen and helium. Yet the chemistry upon which life depends
is ultimately the chemistry of carbon, and there is only one place
in the whole universe where carbon can be created: inside stars. If
the fundamental constants of nature were not what they actually are,
stars might never have formed. The heavier elements on which life
depends—such as carbon, nitrogen, and oxygen—were all created
within stellar cores.

So how are we to account for the origins of life? Nobody really
knows the answer to this question. What can be said, however, is that
biochemically critical elements such as carbon, nitrogen, and oxygen
did not form, and could not have formed, in the early history of the
universe. Their existence is the consequence of the "clumping" or
"accretion" of material into stars, with the subsequent initiation of
nuclear fusion reactions. Carbon is essential to life. Yet its origins
depend totally on how the universe developed after the big bang.
The ratio of the gravitational binding force to rest-mass energy is
such that it permitted the gradual "clumping" of material into larger
bodies: the stars. Stars form as a result of turbulence in giant clouds
of matter within the tenuous interstellar medium. All the heavier elements of the universe, from carbon upward, are believed to be the
result of nuclear fusion within stars, and not to be a direct outcome of

the primordial fireball. Without the formation of stars, the universe would have been limited to hydrogen and helium, with only a tiny percentage of other elements, such as lithium and beryllium.[1]

The nucleosynthesis of carbon, nitrogen, and oxygen must therefore be regarded as essential to the emergence of life. The formation of carbon requires the fusion of three helium nuclei (also known as "alpha-particles"), through a twofold process involving the element beryllium as an intermediate. Two helium nuclei initially fuse to form beryllium, which then captures a third helium nucleus to create carbon. We can set this out technically as follows:

$$^4He + {}^4He \rightarrow {}^8Be$$
$$^8Be + {}^4He \rightarrow {}^{12}C$$

This fusion process occurs rapidly only at very high temperatures in stellar interiors having a high helium abundance. The probability of such a double fusion is very low, since ^8Be is a very unstable and short-lived nucleus. This could lead to a "beryllium bottleneck," preventing the production of heavier nuclei, including oxygen, which would result from the fusion of a carbon nucleus with a further helium nucleus, as follows:

$$^{12}C + {}^4He \rightarrow {}^{16}O$$

Yet if all the ^{12}C was converted to ^{16}O, carbon would not be produced in sufficient quantities to allow for the emergence of life.

In what is recognizably an anthropic argument, the astronomer Fred Hoyle argued during the 1950s that there had to be a yet-undiscovered aspect of the nuclear chemistry of carbon that would allow the production of carbon and oxygen in comparable biophilic quantities. There had to be some yet-undiscovered secret about the deep structure of carbon which accounted for this. The secret was subsequently discovered by William Fowler, who investigated the matter at Hoyle's request. It turned out that the energy levels of oxygen and carbon nuclei were "just right" to allow both to form in the proportions necessary for carbon-based life forms, such as those which we know.

In a later reflection, Hoyle mused about the possible theological implications of this remarkable observation:

From 1953 onward, Willy Fowler and I have always been intrigued by the remarkable relation of the 7.65 MeV [million electron volts] energy level in the nucleus of ^{12}C to the 7.12 MeV level in ^{16}O. If you wanted to produce carbon and oxygen in roughly equal quantities by stellar nucleosynthesis, these are the two levels you would have to fix, and your fixing would have to be just where these levels are actually found to be. Another put-up job? Following the above argument, I am inclined to think so. A commonsense interpretation of the facts suggests that a superintellect has monkeyed with physics, as well as with chemistry and biology, and that there are no blind forces worth speaking about in nature.[2]

The origins of life are thus unquestionably anthropic. They depend upon the fundamental values of constants of nature being such that the universe is able to progress beyond the formation of atomic hydrogen and thus bring about the nucleosynthesis of biologically critical elements. If they had been otherwise, this process might never have begun.

No life forms are known that are based solely upon hydrogen, helium, or lithium—the three lightest elements, all of which were created in the primordial big bang. The big bang, in itself and of itself, was not capable of producing the elements upon which life depends: carbon, nitrogen, and oxygen. Stellar nucleosynthesis is required for their production, which in turn depends upon the clumping of matter after the big bang to form stars. The formation of stars depends upon the value of the gravitational constant, which is regularly cited as an example of fine-tuning. Similarly, the strong nuclear force defines how firmly atomic nuclei bind together and hence the extent to which stars can transmute hydrogen into atoms of the heavier elements. Its value is of critical importance if nucleosynthesis is to take place in stellar interiors.

Yet it is not simply the origins of the universe that seem to show evidence of fine-tuning. A good case can be made for the same patterns emerging at the biological level.[3] It is generally agreed that living systems require two fundamental components: (1) a self-maintaining metabolic system and (2) a genetic system capable of transmitting biological information. Both of these turn out to be critically dependent on the properties of certain chemical elements, which could have been very different.

In recent years, a new field of research has opened up, exploring the remarkable role played in the development of life by metal ions. The term "bioinorganic chemistry" is sometimes used to refer to the exploration of the remarkable biological significance of small traces of metal ions in critical processes, such as photosynthesis and oxygen transport. This field was pioneered in the 1950s by R. J. P. Williams at Oxford University: since then it has become a leading area of scientific research.[4] If the chemical properties of the elements were slightly different, many of the key chemical reactions on which life depends could not take place. The conversion of light to chemical energy in photosynthesis, and the "fixation" of atmospheric nitrogen by plants to produce essential nutrients—these are examples of critical chemical processes upon which life depends. If the fundamental properties of the elements of the universe were different, these reactions might not be able to take place, and life as we know it could not have emerged.

Furthermore, it is clear that a capacity to encode information is of decisive importance for evolution in general and evolvability in particular. And that is critically dependent upon the organic chemistry of carbon, which permits the formation of long, stable chains. No other element has this property; without it, complex molecules essential to life such as RNA (ribonucleic acid) and DNA (deoxyribonucleic acid) would be impossible, as would the replicative processes they control. The capacity of evolution to fine-tune itself is thus ultimately dependent on fundamental chemical properties which in themselves can thus be argued to represent a case of robust and fruitful fine-tuning.

This point is consistently overlooked in many accounts of evolution, which seem to treat physics and chemistry as essentially irrelevant background information to a discussion of evolution. Yet before life can begin, let alone evolve, this biological process requires the availability of a stable planet, irradiated by an energy source capable of chemical conversion and storage, and the existence of a diverse array of core chemical elements with certain fundamental properties. Biology has become so used to the existence and aggregation of highly organized attributes that they are seen primarily as core assumptions of evolutionary theory, rather than something that requires explanation in its own right. There is an implicit assumption that life would adapt to whatever hand of physical and chemical cards were dealt it. Yet this is untested and intrinsically questionable. The emergence of life cannot be studied in isolation from the environment that creates the conditions and provides the resources that make this possible.

So how are these observations to be explained and their significance to be assessed? For the theist, unsurprisingly, these observations point to the inherent potentiality with which the Creator has endowed creation. The relatively recent and unexpected discovery of anthropic phenomena has led to considerable discomfort on the part of some cosmologists, who are uneasy that a new lease of life has been given to discussion of apparent design in the cosmos. This has led to intense discussion of possible explanations of these observations, sometimes driven as much by the hope of eliminating the new styles of natural theology that have emerged in recent years as by the yearning to understand the cosmos better.

It is quite clear that anthropic phenomena fit easily and naturally into a theistic framework, especially its Trinitarian forms. Theologians do not hold that the Christian doctrine of God allows us to predict the specifics of the universe; the general view has always been that, since God made the cosmos with no constraining influences other than the divine will and nature, it could have been created in a variety of manners. René Descartes (1596–1650) thus argued that we must use empirical evidence to determine the structure of the world. There is no question of predicting the form of the world on theological grounds; rather, the form of the world is a contingency which is to be determined empirically and then shown to be consistent with the known will of God.

> There is no question of predicting the form of the world on theological grounds; rather, the form of the world is a contingency which is to be determined empirically and then shown to be consistent with the known will of God.

The observation of anthropic phenomena is thus situated within a long tradition of theological and metaphysical reflection on God as an explanation of the universe. It holds that the general phenomenon of fine-tuning is consonant with Christian belief in a creator God, arguing that the nature of things is such that the most appropriate outcome for a natural theology is to demonstrate that observation of the natural world furnishes conceptual resonance with the Christian vision of God, but not deductive proof of that vision. On this approach, theism offers the best "empirical fit" of the various theories which set out to account for anthropic phenomena. Yet it must be emphasized that Christian theology has never seen itself as charged with the task of inventing an explanation for these observations; rather, they fit within, and resonate with, an *existing* way of thinking, which proves capable of satisfactorily incorporating such observations.

God, then, unquestionably represents a plausible explanation of anthropic phenomena. But is this the *best* explanation? We can't be sure. Alternative perspectives certainly exist. For example, some argue that apparent cosmic fine-tuning is nothing more than an interesting happenstance, a delightful fluke. The fundamental constants in question had to have *some* value—so why not these values? They need possess no further significance. To give an example: the population of the United States of America is a bit over 300 million. There is only one president. The odds of any one American becoming president are thus about one in three hundred million. But so what? Someone has to be president. It may be highly improbable that any given individual should be president, but it is a certainty that someone will be.

Yet this presidential analogy is clearly invalid. The rules of the game are that *somebody* has to be president of the United States. But the universe didn't have to come into being. It's the fact that it's here, as much as the fact that it is highly improbable, which calls out for explanation. In any case, the "biofriendliness" we observe in the universe is far in excess of what is needed to give rise to a few observers like us. If it were the result of random processes, we might expect the observed universe to be minimally rather than optimally biofriendly. But the degree of biofriendliness seems to exceed that in many ways.

Another approach has generated considerable interest: the multiverse. On this view, a multiplicity of universes exist, so that the one we inhabit is an inevitability. We happen to live in a universe with these biologically friendly properties; we do not observe other universes, where these conditions do not pertain. Our insights are restricted by observation-selection effects, which means that our location within a biophilic universe inclines us to propose that the entire cosmos possesses such properties, when in fact other universes will exist which are inimical to life. Indeed, such biophobic universes are predicted to be the norm. We happen to exist in an exceptional universe. On this model, our observable and life-friendly universe is just one of many, a miniscule region or "bubble" within this vast spatial structure of multiple universes.

At present, the multiverse hypothesis remains little more than a fascinating yet highly speculative mathematical exercise. It has, perhaps unwisely, been adopted by atheists anxious to undermine the potential theological significance of fine-tuning in the universe. Thus part of the attraction of the multiverse hypothesis to atheistic physicists such as Steven Weinberg and Leonard Susskind seems to be that it appears to avoid any inference of design or divinity. In fact, however, substantially the same arguments can be brought to bear for the existence of God in the case of a multiverse as in that of a universe, with the multiverse hypothesis being consistent with a theistic understanding of God, not the intellectual defeater of that understanding.[5]

Let's consider this possibility of the multiverse in more detail. If valid, it means that there is no universal set of laws governing the totality of reality. The laws of physics we observe in our universe are not universal, but are more like local by-laws, valid only in our own locality. This immediately raises some difficult questions about the universality of natural science, which increasingly becomes seen as a local, rather than a cosmic, enterprise. To understand the universe we know, we have to propose something outside our universe to explain it. In this case, the explanation takes the form of an unexplained universe-generating and law-generating mechanism, not to mention a vast array of invisible universes. These cannot be seen or proved. In terms of its structure, this argument is remarkably like the Christian claim that an unexplained transcendent God is the ultimate ground and explanation of all things. Those who appeal to God and those who appeal to the multiverse both seek a final explanation of the universe from outside.

So where does this leave us? As I have stressed, the fine-tuning of the universe *proves* nothing. But it resonates strongly with the Christian vision of reality, fitting easily and naturally into the map of reality which emerges from the Christian faith. The capacity of Christianity to map these phenomena is not conclusive proof of anything. It is, however, highly suggestive. It is one among many clues, accumulating to give an overall big picture of reality. It is one among many threads which can be woven together to yield a patterned tapestry. Fine-tuning is a clue to the meaning of the universe, insignificant in isolation, but richly suggestive when set alongside other such clues—some of which we shall consider in what follows.

Chapter 10

The Accidents of Biological History?

*I*t is widely held, especially by atheist evolutionary biologists, that Darwin's theory of evolution destroys any notion of divine design or human purpose. Everything in life is a matter of chance, the random outcome of happenstance. This viewpoint is relentlessly propagated in today's media and is regularly encountered in popular debates.[1] After Darwin, we are regularly told, the idea of divine design has to be abandoned. Biological evolution is a random process, with random outcomes. And that's the end of the matter. It is impossible to speak of "design" in nature after Darwin. Now if you say something often enough, people begin to believe it. But are things really quite as straightforward as this?[2]

Let's begin by making a critical distinction between two senses of the word "Darwinism": Darwinism, considered as a provisional scientific theory about the origins of species, open to revision over time; and Darwinism, considered as a "meta-narrative" or worldview—a grand theory of reality, which is permanently true. The New Atheism treats Darwinism as a meta-narrative, offering a total view of reality.[3] Richard Dawkins, for example, suggests that Darwinism is a "universal and timeless" principle, capable of being applied throughout the universe. In comparison, rival worldviews such as Marxism are to be seen as "parochial and ephemeral."[4] For Dawkins and Daniel Dennett, Darwinism provides a "big picture" of reality, from which any notions of transcendence, purpose, design, or divinity have been eliminated. Yet Darwin did not take this view, and neither do those who stick to rigorously scientific analysis. The problems start when

74

enthusiastic New Atheists start tacking on their metaphysical dogmas and try to pass these off as science.

So what if we limit ourselves to what science actually discloses, instead of smuggling in atheistic ideas and trying to invest them with the cultural authority of science. Does this allow us to speak of design or purpose in the natural world—a notion often expressed using the term "teleology"? At first sight, there is a major problem here. After all, Thomas H. Huxley (1825–95)—widely known as "Darwin's bulldog"—remarked that, having just finished reading Darwin's *Origin of Species* for the first time, he was convinced that "teleology, as commonly understood, had received its deathblow at Mr. Darwin's hands."[5] By "teleology," Huxley meant "goal-directed behaviour" or "progressing towards a purpose or goal." Huxley, unlike Dawkins, was not a doctrinaire atheist.[6] At this point, however, he seems to endorse Dawkins's views.

Yet on a closer reading of Darwin, Huxley changed his mind. Darwin's theories had not eliminated belief in God or belief in teleology. In his 1887 lecture "On the Reception of the *Origin of Species*," Huxley forcefully rebuts three common criticisms, each of which he holds to rest on a serious misrepresentation of Darwin's theory of natural selection.[7] Strikingly, some of these misunderstandings recur in recent atheistic manifestos, such as Dawkins's *God Delusion* (2006) and Dennett's *Darwin's Dangerous Idea* (1995).

1. "It is said that [Darwin] supposes variations to come about 'by chance,' and that the fittest survive the 'chances' of the struggle for existence, and thus 'chance' is substituted for providential design." Huxley argues that Darwin has been grossly misunderstood at this point. Darwin was declaring that he did not know what had caused certain things to happen, while locating such events firmly within the context of the laws of causality. Within a Reformed theological framework, for example, "random" can be translated as "nonpredictable," and thus contextualized within a generalized doctrine of divine providence.

2. "A second very common objection to Mr. Darwin's views was [and is], that they abolish Teleology, and eviscerate the argument from design." This view, of course, is widely repeated in atheistic writings of the late twentieth and early twenty-first centuries, and

it is important to note Huxley's rather different assessment of the situation. Huxley is quite clear that *traditional* approaches to teleology, such as that adopted by William Paley, face a severe challenge from Darwin's account of evolution. Yet the theory of evolution, he argues, bears witness to a "wider teleology," deeply rooted in the structure of the universe. Darwin forced the redefinition of the idea of teleology, not its abandonment.

3. Finally, Huxley addresses the question of whether Darwin's theory is anti-theistic. Having shown that Darwin's theory is not determined by "the belief in chance and the disbelief in design," Huxley argues that it is obvious that "the doctrine of Evolution is neither Anti-theistic nor Theistic." Darwinism has not raised any new problems for theism: the problems of relating God to action in the world were already well known. "In respect of the great problems of Philosophy, the post-Darwinian generation is, in one sense, exactly where the pre-Darwinian generations were."

Huxley's take on things is quite different from that of writers such as Daniel Dennett and Richard Dawkins, who argue that Darwin destroyed belief in any kind of teleology, sweeping away belief in God as outmoded nonsense.[8] Darwin clearly did not believe that himself, and neither did Thomas Huxley, his chief interpreter.

The issue has not gone away. Some Christians have rejected the notion of biological evolution, partly out of concern that it is incompatible with the idea of divine creation and providence. It is certainly true that many evolutionary biologists reject the idea that evolution can be considered in any sense to be teleological. The rejection of any form of teleology achieved the status of an axiomatic truth within neo-Darwinism from about 1970. Evolution was to be understood as an open-ended and indeterminate process, without any predetermined goal. This idea was developed by the French atheistic biologist Jacques Monod (1910–76), who argued that *teleonomy* had displaced *teleology* in evolutionary biology.[9] In using this term, Monod wished to highlight that evolutionary biology was concerned with identifying and clarifying the mechanisms underlying the evolutionary process. Although the mechanisms which governed evolution were of interest, they had no goal. It was impossible to speak meaningfully of "purpose" within evolution. Needless to say, this idea was seized upon by atheistic apologists.[10]

Yet the tide has turned in the last decades. It is now widely accepted that some notion of teleology is essential to make sense of what is observed in nature. This does not amount to the endorsement of traditional Christian notions of design or purpose in nature; it does, however, undermine the simplistic slogan "Darwinism defeats teleology," so characteristic of some recent atheistic writers. Thus the biologist Francisco Ayala argues that the notion of teleological explanation is actually fundamental to modern biology. It is required to account for the familiar functional roles played by parts of living organisms, and to describe the goal of reproductive fitness which plays such a central role in accounts of natural selection. "The use of teleological explanations in biology is not only acceptable but indeed indispensable."[11]

Ernst Mayr (1904–2005), widely credited with inventing the modern philosophy of biology, especially of evolutionary biology, concurs. While recognizing some objections to the use of teleological language in biology,[12] Mayr notes that biologists continue to use teleological language, insisting that it is methodologically and heuristically appropriate and helpful. As Mayr rightly points out, nature abounds in processes and activities that lead to an end or goal. However we choose to interpret them, examples of goal-directed behaviour are widespread in the natural world; indeed, "the occurrence of goal-directed processes is perhaps the most characteristic feature of the world of living systems." Mayr thus insists that "the use of so-called 'teleological' language by biologists is legitimate." In many ways, Mayr here echoes the views of Thomas Huxley, set out a century earlier.

So is there a directionality implicit within evolution, whether one chooses to interpret this teleologically or not? This particular phrasing makes it clear that we are posing a legitimate scientific question, not a speculative theological one. The view that evolution is open-ended, without predictabilities and indeterminate in terms of its outcomes, has achieved a dominant position in evolutionary biology. Many writers who adopt the standard Darwinian paradigm argue for the essentially random and contingent nature of the evolutionary process.

The celebrated evolutionary biologist Stephen Jay Gould (1941–2002) insisted that "almost every interesting event of life's history falls into the realm of contingency."[13] It is pointless to talk about purpose, historical inevitability, or direction. From its beginning to its end, the evolutionary process is governed by contingencies. "We are the accidental result of an unplanned process, . . . the fragile result of an enormous concatenation of improbabilities, not the predictable product of any definite process." As Gould famously put this point, using the characteristically 1990s' analogy of a videotape, if we were to replay the tape of evolutionary history, we would not see the same thing happen each time. "Run the tape again and the first step from prokaryotic to eukaryotic cell may take 12 billion years instead of two." The influence of contingency is such that what happens is the product of happenstance. "Alter any early event, ever so slightly and without apparent importance at the time, and evolution cascades into a radically different channel." Gould argues that the role of contingency in biological evolution is so substantial that the tape will disclose different patterns on each individual replay. So is the process of biological development really so subject to the happenstances of history?

Yet Gould's emphasis on historical contingency is regarded with suspicion by many within the professional community of evolutionary biologists. The Cambridge palaeobiologist Simon Conway Morris, for example, takes a significantly different approach. For Gould, "the awesome improbability of human evolution" is a result of contingency in adaptive evolution. Conway Morris argues against this, challenging the "dominance of contingency."[14]

Conway Morris argues that the number of evolutionary end points is limited. "Rerun the tape of life as often as you like, and the end result will be much the same."[15] *Life's Solution* builds a forceful case for the predictability of evolutionary outcomes, not in terms of genetic details but rather their broad phenotypic manifestations. Convergent evolution is to be understood as "the recurrent tendency of biological organization to arrive at the same solution to a particular need."

Conway Morris's case is based on a thorough and systematic compilation of examples of convergent evolution, in which two or more lineages have independently evolved similar structures and functions. His examples range from the aerodynamics of hovering moths and hummingbirds to the use of silk by spiders and some insects to capture prey. "The details of convergence actually reveal many of the twists and turns of evolutionary change as different starting points are transformed towards common solutions via a variety of well-trodden paths."[16] And what is the significance of convergent evolution? Conway Morris is clear: it reveals the existence of stable regions in biological space. "Convergence occurs because of 'islands' of stability."

The force of Conway Morris's critique of Gould cannot be overlooked. Though contingency is a factor in the overall evolutionary mechanism, it plays a significantly less decisive role than Gould allows. Evolution regularly appears to "converge" on a relatively small number of possible outcomes. Convergence is widespread, despite the infinitude of genetic possibilities, because "the evolutionary routes are many, but the destinations are limited." Certain evolutionary destinations are precluded by "the howling wildernesses of the maladaptive," where the vast majority of genotypes are non-viable, thus precluding further exploration by natural selection. Biological history shows a marked tendency to repeat itself, with life demonstrating an almost eerie ability to find its way to the correct solution, repeatedly. "Life has a peculiar propensity to 'navigate' to rather precise solutions in response to adaptive challenges."

Even what seems to be a random search process will end up identifying stable outcomes in biological space. Although the means of finding such islands of stability may seem erratic, its outcome is ultimately entirely intelligible. Conway Morris suggests that there is a parallel here with the discovery of Easter Island by the Polynesians, perhaps 1,200 years ago.[17] Easter Island is one of the most remote places on earth, at least 3,000 kilometres from the nearest population centres, Tahiti and Chile. Yet though surrounded by the vast, empty wastes of the Pacific Ocean, it was nevertheless discovered by Polynesians. Is this, asks Conway Morris, to be put down to chance and happenstance? Possibly. But probably not. Conway Morris points to the "sophisticated search strategy of the Polynesians" which made its discovery inevitable. The same, he argues,

> Biological history shows a marked tendency to repeat itself, with life demonstrating an almost eerie ability to find its way to the correct solution, repeatedly.

happens in the evolutionary process: "Isolated 'islands' provide havens of biological possibility in an ocean of maladaptedness." It is these "islands of stability" which give rise to the phenomenon of convergent evolution.

The observation that evolutionary biology must explain is the apparent ability of the evolutionary search process to navigate its way to find stable regions of biological space. It is very difficult to see how even a minimalist teleological language can be avoided. Thus Conway Morris suggests, using the image of "Darwin's compass":

> The view that evolution is open-ended, without predictabilities and indeterminate in terms of outcomes[,] is negated by the ubiquity of evolutionary convergence. The central point is that because organisms arrive repeatedly at the same biological solution, the camera-eyes of vertebrates and cephalopods perhaps being the most famous example, this provides not only a degree of predictability but [also] more intriguingly points to a deeper structure to life, a metaphorical landscape across which evolution must necessarily navigate.[18]

Ernst Mayr and other philosophers of biology are right to protest against any attempt to impose a predetermined teleology upon a scientific account of the evolutionary process. Yet Mayr's arguments really only have force when directed against a priori concepts of teleology, which are imported into biology from non-empirical metaphysical systems, whether theist or atheist. Yet it is now widely agreed that some notion of teleology emerges from the study of the evolutionary process itself. Such a teleology is empirical, grounded in a posteriori discernment, not a priori imposition. It is abducted from the observation of the evolutionary process, not deduced from a non-empirical metaphysical system. The term "teleology" is thus rather more elastic than its critics appear to realize. It requires modification in the light of the empirical evidence, not abandonment in response to the somewhat premature and dogmatic demands of those who maintain its inconceivability. This concept of teleology can be mapped onto a Christian framework of understanding, shaped by the core notion of divine providence.

Some Christians will wish to argue for a much more robust statement of the concept of design or the notion of divine providence than those so briefly considered in this chapter. Yet my concern here has been primarily not to articulate a full Christian theology of creation or providence, but to observe how evolutionary biology itself has moved away from the simplistic rejection of apparent purpose or direction within the natural world. Dawkins and Dennett believe that Darwinism tears up the Christian map of reality. That's one way of looking at things. As the evidence of this chapter makes clear, however, the biological world remains open to interpretation in terms of traditional Christian themes of creation and providence, including the notion of design.[19]

So what else can be accommodated within the Christian framework? We have focused on contemporary scientific developments, partly because many wrongly believe that science and faith are implacably opposed. But what of other areas of life and thought? In the next few chapters, we shall explore how the Christian map helps make sense of other core areas of human experience. We begin by reflecting on how human history and culture fit into this scheme of things.

Chapter 11

History, Culture, and Faith

*T*he great English essayist William Hazlitt (1778–1830) once penned some words that are both witty and disturbing. "Man is the only animal that laughs and weeps; for he is the only animal that is struck with the difference between what things are and what they ought to be."[1] We seem to have an inbuilt realization that things are not what they ought to be. We feel the pain of the tension between what we observe and that for which we hope. Why is there so much wrong with the world?

The New Atheism has an easy answer: *religion.* Get rid of religion, and the world would be a better place. "Religion poisons everything" is a rhetorically charged message, which appeals to a certain type of middle-class liberal rationalist. The faults of the world are to be laid at the door of backward-looking superstitions which hold the world back from its rational and scientific destiny. Eliminate religion and the world will be a better place. Religion has led only to violence, intellectual dishonesty, oppression, and social division.

The New Atheism vigorously asserts the fundamental moral and intellectual autonomy of humanity. Human beings are intelligent and rational beings, who can shake off superstitious beliefs and exult in the triumph of reason and science. But where do these beliefs come from? If there is no God, it follows that religion is the creation of human beings. Christopher Hitchens and Richard Dawkins excoriate what they see as the delusional, irrational, and immoral lies of religion. Yet from their atheist perspective, these ideas were invented by human beings—the same human beings whom they exalt as models of rationality and morality. Hitchens appeals to human rationality and morality in making his case for atheism; yet that same rationality and morality gave rise to religious ideas and values which he regards as degenerate, pathological, and oppressive. If there is no God, then the same human nature that invented science (which Dawkins likes) also invented religion (which he does not). This does not bode well for atheism's belief in the fundamental goodness and rationality of humanity.

Religion is therefore the serpent in the rationalist garden of Eden, the seducer of otherwise reasonable people. The contradictions and failures of recent "enlightened" human history—which include the awkward arrival of Nazism and Stalinism, not to mention weapons of mass destruction—are put down, somewhat implausibly, to the resurgence of religion. Not even the rhetorical skills of the greatest New Atheists have been able to weave Stalinism into their narrative of the obstinate persistence of religious belief. The real problem for secular rationalists is that having made human beings the "measure of all things" (Alexander Pope), they find themselves embarrassed by the wide range of beliefs which human beings have chosen to hold—most notably, a widespread belief in God.

If belief in God is a human invention, and if the alleged crimes committed in the name of religion are thus of human origin, then humanity appears to be rather less rational than the New Atheists' worldview allows. The New Atheism criticizes religion as the enemy of humanity, hoping that nobody will notice that their own theory holds it to be a human creation. If religion is evil, as the lazy and loose rhetoric of the New Atheism insists, does not this imply that its creators are also evil? What if human nature is flawed?

It is a thought that cuts to the core of the almost dogmatic belief in the fundamental goodness of human nature that is characteristic of recent atheistic writings. The Enlightenment had a thoroughly optimistic view of human nature: we are good people, who do good things. Or do we? From a Christian perspective, human nature is frail, easily led astray, and prone to sin. Tennyson's famous words in his great poem *Guinevere* often seem hopelessly optimistic and idealistic: "We needs must love the highest when we see it." Does this bear any relationship to the realities of actual human experience?

In a letter of 1887, Lord Acton famously observed that "power tends to corrupt, and absolute power corrupts absolutely." From this, he drew the conclusion that "great men are almost always bad men." It is an idea that has become part of the settled assumptions that govern our thinking about public office and the risks of concentrating too much power in too few hands. The British prime minister William Pitt made a similar comment a century earlier, perhaps drawing on his own experiences in government: "Unlimited power is apt to corrupt the minds of those who possess it." The idea, here focused so pointedly, is that an essentially benign human nature is corrupted by power. The natural goodness of humanity is placed under such severe stress by the temptations and privileges of power that it mostly proves incapable of resisting the shadowy side of this poisoned chalice.

Yet this idea of power corrupting innocent, well-meaning people is only one way of looking at this matter. There is an ancient Anglo-Saxon proverb, preserved in a collection in Durham Cathedral, which offers a more disturbing way of considering the influence of power on human nature. A literal translation of this proverb would be: "Man does as he is when he can do want he wants."[2] In plain English, it means: "We show what we are really like when we can do what we really want." In other words, when all constraints are removed, when there is no accountability or limitations, we behave according to our true natures rather than according to what we think others might expect of us. When we are absolutely free, we are absolutely true to our natures. The possession of absolute power thus allows us to behave as we really are.

It is a very troubling thought. Power, on this reading of things, does not tend to *corrupt*. It tends to *expose*—to bring out what is already there, but which is suppressed through the force of social convention or the need to conform to customs and expectations. On this view, power is a mirror of the soul, a diagnostic tool which reveals what we are really like. What is most disturbing of all is that we may not realize our true natures until we are put in a situation when those limits are finally removed. Readers of William Golding's *Lord of the Flies* (1954) will recognize the point immediately. We might long to be good and to do good, yet we often seem to end up in a very different place.

This is why Hazlitt's words, quoted at the beginning of this chapter, demand careful engagement. How can we make sense of the vast gulf "between what things are and what they ought to be"? Human history is littered with bright hopes and dismal failures; with technological inventions that could have ended war and suffering, yet which seem to end up being used to promote them; with dreams that turn to nightmares. How are we to make sense of this enigma? What is it about human nature that seems to destroy paradise? What "big picture" of human nature helps us make sense of the worrying patterns of history?

To begin with, let us consider how we might make sense of the progress of history and the distinctive features of human culture. A number of controlling narratives have been proposed to make sense of these. One of them, favoured by the New Atheism, is that of the progressive improvement of the human condition through the erosion of religious superstition, and the emancipation of humanity from all taboos and arbitrary limits. It has become much more difficult to sustain this meta-narrative in the West recently, as the manifest failings of Western liberalism have become increasingly clear. Indeed, it is significant that this meta-narrative is one of the chief targets of Terry Eagleton's recent withering critique of the New Atheism.

Eagleton describes the "dream of untrammeled human progress" as a "bright-eyed superstition,"[3] a fairy tale which lacks any rigorous or defensible evidential base. "If ever there was a pious myth and a piece of credulous superstition, it is the liberal-rationalist belief that, a few hiccups apart, we are all steadily en route to a finer world." In the end, it turned out that the Enlightenment articulated ideals that could neither be justified intellectually nor achieved practically.[4] It is thus somewhat perplexing that Christopher Hitchens ends his polemic against religion with a simplistic plea for a return to the Enlightenment, especially the form it took in the eighteenth century.[5] Peter Atkins, another dogmatic atheist, argues that "atheism, and its justification through science, is the apotheosis of the Enlightenment."[6] This sounds depressingly like the kind of propaganda developed by the League of Militant Atheists in the Soviet Union during the 1930s, which called on Soviet citizens to embrace a progressive, scientific, and atheistic worldview.[7] Yet we are surely called to question such fictions about both human individuals and society—including the myth of a lost golden age of science and reason. Why does Hitchens not confront the many recent critics of the Enlightenment, who accuse it of fostering oppression and intolerance—precisely the charges that Hitchens directs against religion?

The New Atheism often accuses those who believe in God of holding on to "unevidenced beliefs," in contrast to the rigorously proven factual statements of enlightened atheists. Yet what of the New Atheists' own belief in human progress? Eagleton dismisses this myth as a demonstrably false pastiche, a luminous example of "blind faith."[8] What rational soul would sign up to such a secular myth, which is obliged to treat such human-created catastrophes as Hiroshima, Auschwitz, and apartheid as "a few local hiccups" which in no way discredit or disrupt the steady upward progress of history? The difference between Christianity and the New Atheism seems to lie in their choice of "unevidenced beliefs" and "controlling myths" (in the New Atheists' language). Neither can be proved; this, however, does not prevent us from making an adjudication as to which appears to be the more reliable and compelling.

So what of a Christian reading of culture and history? It lies beyond the scope of this book to develop even the outline of a Christian philosophy of history; what I can briefly do, however, is to note some themes of such a way of looking at history and culture and explore how they map onto what we actually observe. Two controlling themes here are the ideas of humanity in the first place as created in the "image of God," and in the second place as sinful. While theologians and religious communities differ in the relative emphasis placed upon these two elements of a Christian understanding of human nature, they are nevertheless twin poles around which any try to make sense of the enigmas and puzzles of how we behave, as individuals and in society.

We find ourselves excited and inspired by the vision of God, which draws us upward; we find ourselves pulled down by the frailty and fallenness of human nature. It is a familiar dilemma, famously articulated by Paul: "I do not do the good I want, but the evil I do not want is what I do" (Rom. 7:19). From a Christian perspective, it is clear that we must at one and the same time recognize a greater destiny or capacity in humanity than most political systems or philosophies allow, and a corresponding capacity to fail to achieve such aspirations. Christian theology gives us a critical lens through which to view the complex motivations and mixed agendas of human beings.

We bear God's image, yet we are sinful. We are capable of good, just as we are capable of evil.

This way of thinking allows us to frame the complex picture we see of human culture and history, characterized by aspirations to greatness and goodness on the one hand, and oppression and violence on the other. Many have commented on the profound ambiguity of history and the havoc which it wreaks for naive theories of the goodness of humanity. Terry Eagleton is one of a series of commentators to point out the darker side of contemporary human culture ("corporate greed, the police state, a politically compromised science, and a permanent war economy") and history ("the misery wreaked by racism and sexism, the sordid history of colonialism and imperialism, the generation of poverty and famine").

> Christian theology gives us a critical lens through which to view the complex motivations and mixed agendas of human beings. We bear God's image, yet we are sinful. We are capable of good, just as we are capable of evil.

As a species, humanity may indeed have the capacity for good; this seems matched, however, by a capacity for evil. A recognition of this profound ambiguity is essential if we are to avoid political and social utopianism, based on naive, ideologically driven, non-empirical value judgements about human nature. As J. R. R. Tolkien, later to achieve fame for his *Lord of the Rings* trilogy, wrote so presciently in 1931, on the eve of the rise of Nazism, a naive view of humanity leads to political utopianism, in which "progress" potentially leads to catastrophe.

> I will not walk with your progressive apes,
> Erect and sapient. Before them gapes
> the dark abyss to which their progress tends.[9]

Nobody yet knew of the depths of depravity and cruelty that would be created by the rise of Nazism and Stalinism in the 1930s. Yet Tolkien rightly and perceptively saw something that most Enlightenment writers failed to see: everything rests on the moral character of human beings. Technological developments can be used to cure or to kill. Sadly, the choice is made by human beings, and the choices they make can be disastrous. Tolkien's *Lord of the Rings* explores these themes with a perception and insight sadly absent from some recent atheist manifestos.

Scientific advance has placed into our hands new technologies and techniques: thus we can do things today that our ancestors could only have dreamed of. Yet this progress raises some real problems. A medical advance that helps us understand how the human body works might lead to new cures; yet it could also lead to a weapon of mass destruction, designed to use this knowledge of human physiology to destroy populations.

Now let me make it clear that there is nothing intrinsically wrong with science. The problem concerns how we, as human beings, choose to use it. How trustworthy are we? Why do we do bad things with inventions that could lead to good outcomes? Why do we keep turning ploughshares into swords?[10] Thoughts like this led the German social philosopher Theodor Adorno (1903–69) to raise some awkward questions about faith in human progress. For Adorno, the "progress" in question was from the sling to the atom bomb.

To explore this point, we shall look at an episode in the career of one of America's greatest scientists, Louis Frederick Fieser (1899–1977), who became professor of chemistry at Harvard University in 1930. He was noted for developing, along with his wife, Mary Peters Fieser (1909–97), the artificial synthesis of a series of important naturally occurring compounds, including vitamin K, necessary for blood coagulation.[11] Fieser's brilliant synthetic procedures made medically important chemicals much cheaper and more widely available, with highly beneficial outcomes for patient care. In this respect, Fieser can be seen as embodying all that is good about science: working for the advancement of humanity.

Fieser also headed a team at Harvard which invented another chemical product during the period 1942–43, which many scientists today prefer to pass over in embarrassed silence. The U.S. Army urgently needed a chemical weapon suitable for burning tracts of jungle and eliminating troops in foxholes in the Pacific war theatre. Fieser and his team developed the mixture of chemicals now known as "napalm," which was deliberately designed to use fire as an effective and destructive weapon of war. Napalm, once ignited, could not be extinguished; it took the form of a gel, which stuck to human bodies and could not be removed; and it rapidly exhausted oxygen, causing death by suffocation if not through burns. It was an ideal weapon in the Pacific theatre of war. Yet its use was not restricted to eliminating troops hidden in foxholes or jungles. On the night of 9–10 March 1945, the U.S. Air Force dropped 1,700 tons of napalm bombs on the city of Tokyo, causing massive loss of civilian life. It is thought that 100,000 people died that night—an immediate loss of life greater than that caused initially by either of the atom bombs dropped a few months later on Hiroshima and Nagasaki.

Justification could be offered for what Fieser did. After all, the United States was engaged in total warfare at the time.[12] The extension of the war might arguably have led to even greater loss of life. Yet when all is said and done, the development of napalm is a reminder that science can be used to kill and destroy humanity, as much as to heal and extend human life. It is a sobering thought, one that does much to undermine the shallow optimism of those who simplistically and naively exalt science as the saviour of humanity.

Again, I emphasize that I make no criticism of scientific progress. My concern is what we, as morally flawed human beings, do with that progress. Who, for example, can overlook the awkward fact that the engine that drives scientific advance is sometimes military—the desire to have better weapons? This was a major concern for Sir Joseph Rotblat (1908–2005), the only physicist to leave the Manhattan Project to create the first atomic bomb on the grounds of conscience, who was awarded the Nobel Peace Prize in 1995.[13] In his acceptance speech, "Remember Your Humanity," Rotblat highlighted the moral ambiguity of humanity and its implications for scientific progress. Rotblat restated his concerns further in 1999:

> To a large extent the nuclear arms race was driven by scientists. They kept on designing new types of weapons, not because of any credible requirement—arsenals a hundred times smaller would have sufficed for any conceivable deterrence purpose—but mainly to satisfy their inflated egos, or for the intense exhilaration experienced in exploring new technical concepts.[14]

My concern here is not to debate the ethics of napalm or nuclear weapons, but to highlight the need for a critical perspective which avoids idealization of any area of professional or political life. A realistic view of human nature is essential to make sense of the failures and foibles evident in the world of politics, business, science, and economics. In no way should the darker side of human nature and undertakings deter us from becoming involved in these areas and working to make things better. Realism about human nature is the precondition for sustained action in these contexts. Otherwise the outcome is delusional or utopian.

The Christian faith thus offers an interpretative lens through which we see human nature as it really is. It helps us make sense of things; but it also helps us avoid naive estimations of human ideals and capacities. Like a skilled physician, Christianity offers a diagnosis of the human situation—not in order to pass judgement and then pass on, but to identify what must be done to transform the situation. Identification of the malady is the essential precondition for a cure. The Christian interpretative lens allows us to work out what is wrong with humanity, before we move on to deal with the solution—a solution articulated in the Christian doctrine of redemption, to which we shall return.

Our attention now turns to another aspect of human nature: the pursuit of things that really matter to us. Though we may be flawed, we have a vision of excellence and fulfilment which makes us yearn to transcend our human limitations. So where do these ideals come from? And where do they lead us? In what follows, we shall consider the deeply evocative human quest for our heart's desire.

Chapter 12

The Heart's Desire

Longing for Significance

*W*e dream of better worlds—worlds of justice, peace, and meaning. The world we see around us often seems to fall short of our aspirations. Somehow, we seem to possess deep intuitions that things shouldn't be like this. As we noted earlier, William Hazlitt poignantly remarked that man "is the only animal that is struck with the difference between what things are and what they ought to be." We observe suffering—and we long for a world in which pain, suffering, and death exist no more. We see injustice—and we long for a world in which righteousness will roll down from the mountains like a stream, sweeping away corruption. Surely there must be more to reality than what we see around us! Surely there must be a better world than this!

Maybe these are just consoling thoughts, psychological defences designed to shield us from the harsh realities of life. Then again, they might be clues. They might point to a voice that is calling us, telling us of another land—a land that we once left behind, or a land that we might hope to inhabit in the future. This was certainly the view of J. R. R. Tolkien, whose detailed study of Norse and Anglo-Saxon epics led him to write *The Lord of the Rings*. Tolkien held that the imagination was the key to meaning, opening up worlds that we were meant to see, and in whose light we could understand the enigmas and riddles of life.

In his poem "Mythopoeia," written in 1931 after a long conversation with C. S. Lewis, Tolkien argues that humanity possesses a homing instinct, an inbuilt sense of our true origins and destiny. The human heart, he wrote, still[1]

draws some wisdom from the only Wise,
and still recalls him.

A similar idea is found in the document "Faith and Reason," issued
by Pope John Paul II in 1998. "God has placed in the human heart a
desire to know the truth." Human beings long to know the truth, and
are constantly searching for it—and in doing so, are led home to God,
the creator and the ultimate goal of humanity. "In the far reaches of
the human heart there is a seed of desire and nostalgia for God."[2]

Tolkien works with a very similar idea. We dream of enchanted
worlds and magic realms, not as a form of escapism, but as a way of
discovering and expressing our true identity and destiny. As Tolkien
concludes:

> Yes! "wish-fulfilment dreams" we spin to cheat
> our timid hearts and ugly Fact defeat!
> Whence came the wish, and whence the power to dream,
> or some things fair and others ugly deem?[3]

We are, Tolkien insists, *meant* to dream and reflect. And what we
create reflects how we are created: "We make still by the law in
which we're made."

So how can we make sense of this deep instinct that there is more
to life than what we see around us? One obvious answer is to dismiss
this intuition as a delusion, a cruel fantasy that we have invented
because we cannot cope with the realities of this meaningless world.
Although this idea can be found in ancient writers, it was developed
by three more recent writers, who each took it in different directions. The German atheist philosopher Ludwig Feuerbach (1804–72)
argued that we project our longings and hopes onto some kind of
imaginary screen and call this imagined reality "God." There is no
god, he declares—only a bundle of human hopes and yearnings,
which naive humans mistake for God.

Karl Marx (1818–83) developed this idea further. We need to
understand why people invent the idea of God in the first place. Marx
argued that the cause of this deluded dream of God is social and economic misery: "Religion is the sigh of the oppressed creature. . . . It is
the opium of the people." When the socialist revolution came, Marx
declared, the cause of belief in God would be removed. Belief in God

would wither away. In fact, it did nothing of the sort. The persistence of belief in God in the Soviet Union and its satellite states was a major headache for Marxist theorists. With the collapse of the Soviet Union, religious belief and practice quickly re-established themselves.

Sigmund Freud (1856–1939) argued that belief in God is an illusion, a "wish-world" resulting from biological and psychological pressures. "Religious beliefs are illusions, fulfilments of the oldest, strongest and most urgent wishes of humanity." God is the great sky father, an imaginary source of an equally imaginary protection and comfort. Belief in God is a dream, a wish-fulfilment, which causes psychological damage to people.

Each of these three approaches shares a common theme: the dream of a better world or a loving God is an invention, a human construction which responds to our intellectual, social, or psychological environment. There is no God, nothing transcendent. There is nothing beyond this visible world. Our dreams of another world are simply naive attempts to console ourselves and protect ourselves from the unbearable truth of meaninglessness. Religion is a consoling delusion, the opium of the people.

The Polish poet Czesław Miłosz (1911–2004), who won the Nobel Prize for Literature in 1980, has an interesting point to make about the delusions of modernity. After finding himself stifled intellectually, first under Nazism and then under Stalinism, Czesław had little doubt about the ultimate source of despair and tyranny in the twentieth century. In a remarkable essay titled "The Discreet Charm of Nihilism," he points out that it is not religion, but its nihilist antithesis, which lies at the root of the century's oppressive totalitarianism:

> Religion, opium for the people! To those suffering pain, humiliation, illness, and serfdom, it promised a reward in afterlife. And now we are witnessing a transformation. A true opium of the people is a belief in nothingness after death—the huge solace of thinking that for our betrayals, greed, cowardice, murders we are not going to be judged.[4]

The Marxist creed has now been inverted. The true opium of modernity is the belief that there is *no* God, so that humans are free to do precisely as they please. We create a moral universe in which we are free to do as we please. There is no ultimate accountability.

These themes have been taken up and developed by many within Western culture, most recently in the New Atheism that developed around 2006, with the publication of Richard Dawkins's *The God Delusion*. The take-home message of this work is simple and direct. Nothing exists outside the natural order, and the most reliable way to understand that order is to apply the scientific method. God is a delusion—an *understandable* delusion, but nonetheless a delusion. Dawkins argues that this delusional belief in God arises from a "meme." As we noted earlier (in chap. 6), the idea of the "meme" itself strikes many people as delusional: it seems to represent blind faith in something for which there is little real evidential support. More than one wit has suggested that Dawkins believes in memes in much the same way he seems to think religionists believe in God.

So is belief in God a delusion? C. S. Lewis certainly thought so as a young man, when he was going through an aggressively atheistic phase. Lewis found himself yearning for a world of passion, beauty, and meaning which he had come to believe did not and could not exist. "Nearly all that I loved I believed to be imaginary; nearly all that I believed to be real I thought grim and meaningless."[5] His imagination told him there was a better world; his reason told him that this was simply nonsense. He therefore believed that he had no option other than to confront the bleakness of a senseless world and his pointless existence. He was forced to choose between an imagined world of beauty and meaning, and an empirical world of futility and hopelessness.

Some will rightly suggest that this represents an unnecessary restriction on possibilities. There might be other ways of making sense of life which accentuate the positives of empirical existence. Yet Richard Dawkins, so diametrically opposed to Lewis on so many issues, would concur with this analysis of the empirical world:

> In a universe of blind physical forces and genetic replication, some people are going to get hurt, other people are going to get lucky, and you won't find any rhyme or reason in it, nor any justice. The universe we observe had precisely the properties we should expect if there is, at bottom, no design, no purpose, no evil and no good, nothing but blind pitiless indifference.[6]

What you see is what you get. There is no evil, no good, and no purpose in this blind and meaningless universe. Dawkins would certainly allow that human beings can—and do—*construct* meaning: indeed, one of his basic arguments against religion is that it constructs an arbitrary and delusional belief in order to try to cope with what is fundamentally a meaningless world.[7] For Dawkins, this belief is whimsically imposed upon the world, not legitimately discerned within it. Belief in God is an invention, not an authentic discovery or revelation of reality.

Lewis, however, argued that our longing for significance is a marker of something that lies beyond the thresholds of our experience. It is a clue which suggests that human beings are created for something better than the world that we know. For Lewis, human longing is primarily concerned with intimating another transcendent world, the inhabitation of which is the ultimate goal of our life. It is only secondarily concerned with the existence of God, even though this transcendent realm is indeed the "kingdom of God." Where Dawkins skims the surface of reality, believing that the superficial appearance of the world is identical with its deep structures, Lewis holds that what we observe is a pointer to something hidden—which, once discovered, changes the way in which we see everything.

Lewis certainly is not alone in having experienced a deep sense of desire for something unknown, possibly unknowable. The English poet Matthew Arnold (1822–88) spoke of German Romantic literature bearing witness to "a wistful, soft, tearful longing," never fully satisfied by the empirical world. Having experienced intense desire himself, Lewis believed that no theory of reality, no worldview, could be adequate unless it had the capacity to accommodate such experiences. How can such an intense desire, such an inconsolable longing, be accounted for? What purpose does it serve when it seems to be directed towards nothing that we have experienced or can imagine?[8] The great French philosopher Blaise Pascal (1623–62) saw human longing as a hint pointing towards our true goal:

> What else does this longing and helplessness proclaim, but that there was once in each person a true happiness, of which all that now remains is the empty print and trace? We try to fill this in vain with everything around us, seeking in things that are not there the help we cannot find in those that are there. Yet nobody can change

things, because this infinite abyss can only be filled with something that is infinite and unchanging—in other words, by God himself. God alone is our true good.[9]

This is an insight that many have found deeply satisfying. And Lewis came to discover this answer after a long period of atheism, during which he persuaded himself that there was no answer to be found.

For many years, Lewis believed that the intense desire that he named "Joy" was simply a desire for something imaginary. Then he began to realize that it might point towards something that was as real as it was significant. At this point, Lewis's transition concerns not the validity or even the nature of this experience, but its significance. What he had initially thought of as an intense yet ultimately meaningless experience came to be seen in a quite different light. It was seen through a new lens, using a new interpretative framework. And its significance altered radically. Here Lewis's reflections on the nature of desire are best thought of as intuitive reflections, rather than a full-blown rational defence of the existence of God. To use the categories devised by the great American philosopher Charles Sanders Peirce (1839–1914), Lewis is clearly using an *abductive* rather than a *deductive* approach. The question he engages is simple: What way of looking at things might be proposed that enables this puzzling observation to be explained?

Lewis argues that most people experience a passionate desire for something that simply cannot be had in this world. So how is this to be explained? Lewis explores three main possibilities in his classic work *Mere Christianity*. Some argue that this failure to find satisfaction and delight arises from desiring the wrong things in the world. Once the correct object of human desire is found, true satisfaction will result. And so they commit themselves to a process of restless questing, which never seems to reach or find its goal. Others try to deny and repress the feeling altogether, dismissing it as merely "wishful thinking" or "adolescent romanticism." Although initially inclined towards the second of these positions, Lewis gradually came to believe that there was a third way of making sense of such a longing: seeing it as a pointer towards another world. "If I find in myself a desire which no experience in this world can satisfy, the most probable explanation is that I was made for another world." We are like a skilfully crafted musical instrument, incomplete in the absence of the player, no matter how finely tuned and beautifully constructed. Its potential to create beauty and joy lies unfulfilled.

Yet we must avoid thinking of Christianity simply as a set of ideas or a network of interlocking and interacting concepts. The Christian faith is indeed about a web of ideas, capable of making sense of what we see around us. Yet the Christian vision of reality goes far beyond the limited realm of ideas: it also embraces images, narratives, and values. For J. R. R. Tolkien, the central theme is that of "myth"—a term by which Tolkien really means what we would now term a "meta-narrative," a story which positions and makes sense of all other stories.[10] A "myth" is thus not to be understood as something which is untrue, as the everyday use of the word might suggest. For Tolkien, a myth is a narrative of origins, actions, and values which gives meaning to events and individuals. It is a vision of reality, refracted through human language and experience.[11]

As illustrated in Tolkien's own writings, such as *The Lord of the Rings*, myths have the power to captivate the human imagination,[12] opening up visions of better and fairer worlds. Tolkien found the notion of a controlling story to be far more powerful and sat-

> The Christian faith is indeed about a web of ideas, capable of making sense of what we see around us. Yet the Christian vision of reality goes far beyond the limited realm of ideas: it also embraces images, narratives, and values.

isfying than a set of ideas. They made a deep appeal to the imagination, offering rich images rather than abstract concepts, descriptions of actions rather than theoretical arguments. Myth, Tolkien came to believe, is essential to human reflection: it governs how we discover our true identity and goal.

Tolkien argued that every culture was founded on an underlying myth: a story that makes sense of history and experience. The modern age is no exception. As Terry Eagleton and other cultural commentators have noted, modernity is based on its own meta-narrative of progress and enlightenment. So how are we to judge these myths, these controlling narratives which set out to make sense of what we see and experience? For Tolkien, the answer lies in the capacity of a myth to explain the enigmas of life. We have already explored something of the ability of the Christian faith to illuminate reality, and even to illuminate its darker recesses.

Yet Tolkien has more to say about the nature of myth. There are many myths, such as the great pagan myths of old and their modern equivalents. Yet each of these myths, he argues, is a reflection or echo of something greater. They are as pieces of glass, refracting a greater light that lies beyond them. All worldviews, whether religious or secular, rest on myths: attempts to account for reality, expressed in many different ways, as splintered fragments of light, each reflecting only some aspects of a greater whole. For Tolkien, Christianity takes the structural form of such a myth. Yet it is the *real* myth, to which all other myths only approximate and aspire. It is the grand narrative, the full picture, which explains and makes sense of other narratives and pictures.

Lewis took a similar view. In a paper titled "Is Theology Poetry?" delivered to the Socratic Club at Oxford in 1945, Lewis insists that occasional similarities between Christianity and other religions are to be expected and welcomed, on the basis of the overarching nature of the Christian view of reality. The Christian faith holds that

> there is some divine illumination vouchsafed to all men. The Divine light, we are told, "lighteneth every man." We should, therefore, expect to find in the imagination of great Pagan teachers and myth-makers some glimpse of that theme which we believe to be the very plot of the whole cosmic story—the theme of incarnation, death and rebirth.[13]

Lewis argues that Christianity offers a grand narrative which makes sense of all things, which gives rise to sub-narratives that are incomplete, occasionally distorted, refractions of its greater whole. The gospel tells the whole truth, the whole story, setting out a narrative account of reality that allows these sub-narratives to be positioned and explained, while indicating that these only find their completion and fulfilment in that one grand narrative of the Christian gospel, in which "Myth became Fact."

It is this gospel meta-narrative, this controlling and illuminating story, Lewis argues, that makes sense of the deep human longing for beauty, significance, and meaning. The Christian narrative of origins and destiny speaks of humanity having been created in order to know God, and thence to come home to the new Jerusalem. Augustine of Hippo (354–430) summarizes this narrative in a famous prayer: "You have made us for you, and our heart is restless until it finds its rest in you."[14] This restlessness is triggered and renewed by an encounter with God's creation, which is richly studded with signs of penultimacy. For the wise, the natural world declares its own limitations and urges us to look *beyond* it by looking *through* it. The created order is like a window, through which glimpses of its creator may be discerned. True meaning is thus to be found elsewhere.

Human beings possess an instinct of transcendence, which is stimulated by memory, beauty, and longing. This homing instinct takes the form of "a desire for our own far-off country."[15] For Lewis, beauty evokes an ideal that is more real than anything we encounter in this transitory world, evoking a sense of longing for a half-remembered realm from which we are presently exiled. It is a desire "for something that has never actually appeared in our experience," yet which is constantly suggested and intimated by what we do experience.

We could develop this idea using Plato's famous image of people trapped for all their lives in an underground cave. They know only a flickering world of shadows cast by the flames of the fire that keeps them warm. Plato wants us to realize that we live in a shadowland. Beyond it lies a world of color, beauty, the babbling of clear mountain streams, and the fresh fragrance of meadow flowers. We will never discover this better world if we dogmatically insist that the shadowland is the only true reality. Those who limit reality to what we see on the surface merely imprison themselves, failing to realize what lies beyond the shadows.[16] To give the image a Christian twist: someone needs to enter the shadowland from the world beyond, tell us about it, and lead us into its light and beauty. Our desire for beauty is a homing instinct for the real world beyond the shadows and smoke of the cave.

Lewis thus argues that the perennial human "quest for beauty" is actually a quest for the *source* of that beauty, which is only mediated through the things of this world. It is not contained within them, nor does it ultimately point towards anything in this world. "The books or the music in which we thought the beauty was located will betray us if we trust to them: it was not *in* them, it only came *through* them, and what came through them was longing."[17] For Lewis, the desire, the sense of longing, remains with us, "still wandering and uncertain of its object." This desire is "a longing to be reunited with something in the universe from which we now feel cut off, to be on the inside of some door which we have always seen from the outside."[18]

So where do we truly belong? Where is our homeland? For Lewis, the heart's desire can never be satisfied by anything that is finite or created. A door must be opened so that we can enter into another world, within which our true satisfaction and joy are to be found. *Yet we do not need to leave this world to pass through that door.* As humans, we live in the tension between the world that we know and one that we do not. The Christian narrative offers multiple perspectives on our situation. It allows us to realize that we are in exile on earth, while we anticipate our return to heaven. It helps us realize that we are in captivity in Egypt, awaiting our entry into the promised land of milk and honey.

Though physically located in one place, we mentally inhabit another, where we believe that we truly belong. "Paradise is our native land" (Cyprian of Carthage, 200–253). We thus have a homing instinct for another world. Or, to use an image found in the writings of the Renaissance poet Francis Quarles (1592–1644), our soul is like an iron needle drawn to the magnetic pole of God. Though we live here on earth, the beauty, joy, and hope of paradise shape our thoughts and actions. The gospel unfolds a story-shaped world which makes sense of the enigmas of our experience—while at the same time offering hope for the future.

Yet our hopes for the future are linked with our understanding of our present situation. As we bring this work to a conclusion, we may reflect further on how the Christian faith transforms us by opening up new ways of understanding our identity, purpose, and value.

Chapter 13

Surprised by Meaning

The French philosopher Blaise Pascal is one of many to ponder the meaning of life. Is it all a short, meaningless accident?

> When I consider the short duration of my life, swallowed up in the eternity before and after, the little space which I fill, and even which I can see, engulfed in the infinite immensity of spaces of which I know nothing, and which do not know me, I am frightened, and am astonished at being here rather than there. For there is no reason why I am here rather than there, why now rather than then. Who has put me here? By whose order and direction have this place and this time been allotted to me?[1]

Pascal spoke of his fear that his brief occupation of a "little space" in the vast history of the universe would be random, accidental, and devoid of meaning. How could he make sense of things?

Reality is open to multiple interpretations. There are different ways of looking at things, with significantly different existential outcomes. Some leave us deeply disturbed, others excite us, some console us. To explore this point, we may consider the night sky. Imagine that you are out on a dark, cold night. Above you, pinpoints of light twinkle in the dark velvet sky. Many have felt overwhelmed by the solemn stillness of the sky at night. But what does it say to us?

It is a question that I have often reflected on myself. When I was nine or ten years old, I managed to build myself a small telescope so I could observe the moons of Jupiter and explore the Milky Way. I spent many a cold winter night staring at the vast expanses of space, wondering where I fitted into all of this. I remember looking at one of the brightest nebulae in the night sky—M31 in Andromeda, now known to be one of the nearest galaxies. Even with my small telescope, I could see something of its beauty. Yet its beauty was tinged with melancholy. I knew that it was more than two million light years away. The light now leaving that distant galaxy would not reach earth for two million years, by which time I would be long since dead. The night sky seemed to me to point to the vastness of the cosmos and the insignificance of humanity.

Much the same thoughts were expressed more recently, though in a much more articulate and reflective manner, by Ursula Goodenough, a cell biologist interested in exploring the deeper meaning of the natural order. She tells of how she became so disturbed by the meaninglessness of the cosmos that she decided to stop thinking about it. "Our sun too will die, frying the Earth to a crisp during its heat-death, spewing its bits and pieces out into the frigid nothingness of curved spacetime."[2] She found herself being overwhelmed by a "bleak emptiness" every time she thought about the deeper meaning of the cosmos. "The night sky was ruined. I would never be able to look at it again." In the end, she decided not to think about such things. She decided to cope with the "the apparent pointlessness of it all" by telling herself that there was no point to seek or to find. As Steven Weinberg once commented, "The more the universe seems comprehensible, the more it seems pointless." The information is there—but it doesn't create a pattern. Nothing seems to fit together. There is no big picture.

The classic way of dealing with this troubling realization is Stoic indifference. We should rise above the meaninglessness of the cosmos and concentrate upon building our own character. We create our own problems through our responses to the world. The wise person cultivates a supreme indifference and disengagement from reality, concentrating on the formation of personal character and rationality.[3] Instead of trying to make sense of a senseless universe, the wise person constructs a private rational universe of meaning and value. The development of character is thus an assertion of the individual's capacity to create meaning in the face of a meaningless world. Similar ideas are widely encountered today. Many argue that we must construct our own worlds of meaning, assembling ideas and values into a patchwork quilt of meaning, tailored to our own needs and concerns.

There is, however, an alternative way of looking at things which goes back to the dawn of civilization. Where the New Atheism skims the surface of reality, the wise choose to go deeper. We cannot rest content with a superficial reading of nature. We need to go further and deeper. Meaning, here understood to be embedded deep in the order of things, can be discerned by the wise. It does not need to be constructed or invented; it is already present. The British philosopher and writer Iris Murdoch (1919–99) spoke of "the calming, whole-making tendencies of human thought," by which she means the ability of a "big picture" or "grand narrative" to integrate our vision of reality.

Murdoch is right: we seek meaning in life, rather than endless additional facts about life. It is easy to accumulate information, pasting new items into our mental notebooks in much the same way as a keen stamp collector adds new items to an album. But what purpose does this serve? Earlier we noted how the poet Edna St. Vincent Millay (1892–1950) spoke of "a meteoric shower of facts" raining from the sky, yet lying on the ground, "unquestioned, uncombined." We are overwhelmed with information, as a casual search of the Internet reveals. Yet what bigger picture does this information disclose? What happens when we join together the dots? When we put all the pieces of the jigsaw together? Is there a picture at all? Or is it simply a mass of disconnected bits of information?

Just as the merits of a telescope are judged partly by the clarity with which it allows us to see distant objects, so a worldview is assessed by how well it illuminates the landscape of reality and brings everything into sharp focus. The Christian faith enables us to make sense of things, so that we hear tunes where others only hear noise, and see patterns where others see disorder and chaos. What was once a blurred and fuzzy image is suddenly seen clearly and distinctly.

> "I believe in Christianity as I believe that the Sun has risen, not only because I see it, but because by it, I see everything else." —C. S. Lewis

This is the view that has been explored throughout this work. The Christian faith offers a framework of meaning which is deeply embedded in the order of things and ultimately originates from and expresses the character of God. The world may indeed seem meaningless and pointless. What is needed, however, is a lens or a conceptual framework which brings things into focus. The world may *seem* meaningless; yet this is because we do not see it in the right way. If it seems hopelessly out of focus and disorganized, it is because we have yet to find the key to bringing it into focus and weaving its seemingly disconnected and unrelated threads together into a tapestry of meaning. Christianity provides a framework of meaning which illuminates the shadowlands of reality, brings our observations of the world into focus, and weaves the threads of our experience into a pattern. C. S. Lewis summed it up well in a well-turned statement we noted earlier: "I believe in Christianity as I believe that the Sun has risen, not only because I see it, but because by it, I see everything else."[4]

Yet this framework of meaning is not something that we manage to figure out by ourselves, after an exhaustive analysis of all the options. The meaning that we quest is *disclosed* to us. We are, so to speak, "surprised by meaning." The traditional Christian language of "revelation" affirms that the meaning that all human beings seek, yet find so elusive and mysterious, has been shown to us. Once someone has shown us how to make sense of things, it seems obvious. But we couldn't get there by ourselves. When Thomas H. Huxley first read Darwin's *Origin of Species*, he is reported to have exclaimed: "How stupid of me not to have thought of that!" Once it had been pointed out to him, it made sense of what Huxley had himself observed. *But Huxley had not been able to find the answer for himself.* Someone had to show him how everything was woven together and interconnected. The Christian faith speaks of a God who holds the key to our history and who has entrusted that key to us so that we might unlock the door to the true meaning of things.

So what kind of meaning are we talking about? The social psychologist Roy Baumeister recently set out a significant analysis of theories of the meaning of life, in which he identified what themes had to be engaged and explored before the human quest for meaning could be satisfied.[5] There were, he argued, four fundamental questions that had to be answered convincingly if a way of thinking was to count as a "meaning of life":

1. The question of *Identity*: Who am I?
2. The question of *Value*: Do I matter?

3. The question of *Purpose*: Why am I here?
4. The question of *Agency*: Can I make a difference?

These are not empirical questions, which can be answered by the natural sciences. As we have seen, they lie beyond its intellectual horizons and methodological frontiers. Yet we cannot live without formulating answers to such questions.

For example, consider the question of justice—a passionate concern for many in today's complex and broken world. Yet justice is not something that we can "read off" from the world. Indeed, some recent attempts to ground justice in nature sometimes end up defending the Darwinian idea of the "survival of the fittest."[6] What of widows and orphans? Of the powerless and weak? In his penetrating and highly acclaimed writings on the nature of justice, Michael J. Sandel argues that any notion of justice depends upon competing conceptions of the good life—that is, networks of beliefs about human nature, values, and purpose. Sandel, professor of government at Harvard University, argues that where rationalism held that reason could answer such questions, the harsh reality has turned out to be that they cannot be meaningfully answered without depending upon beliefs that ultimately cannot be proved.[7]

The Enlightenment dream of basing justice on pure reason has foundered. Perhaps more disturbingly for rationalist accounts of reality, such as those favored by the New Atheism, there is a growing consensus among intellectual historians that the Enlightenment was so diverse that it cannot really be spoken of as a single movement. Instead of speaking of human "rationality," we must speak of "rationalities."[8] The Enlightenment turns out to be a rational multiverse, with competing and diverging accounts of the nature and scope of human reason. That's one of the reasons why so many have concluded that the Enlightenment offered theories of rationality and morality which proved impossible to defend in theory, and impossible to implement in practice.[9] When the New Atheism appeals to reason and morality in defending its own ideas and critiquing those of theists, we are perfectly entitled to ask for clarification. Which rationality do you mean? And which morality?[10]

As Sandel rightly points out, public reason is not neutral: it is shaped by a theory of the good. Secular rationalism therefore does not, and *cannot*, provide an adequate foundation for justice. Sandel argues that secular liberalism represents a hollow and shallow view of the world, which ends up merely defending the right of citizens to do whatever they please, as long as they hurt no one else.[11] But real justice is about values and ideals. Secularism often presents itself as offering a "neutral" approach to ethics and social questions, allowing all to share in public debate irrespective of their faith commitments. Sandel argues that this is untenable: secularism denies, excludes, and suppresses the moral ideals and values of others, while maintaining the myth of its own neutrality.

Sandel's analysis highlights the importance of theories of the meaning of life which bestow value and dignity upon actors and actions. We cannot pretend that there is a "neutral" public sphere: all spheres of life are shaped by these theories—including the Christian faith. Christianity does more than make sense of things; it also confers meaning and value. So how does the "big picture" offered by Christianity engage with these fundamental questions? In what follows, we shall explore each of the four issues we noted earlier in this chapter.

1. Identity: Who Am I?

It is very easy to give definitions of human identity. We are defined by our genetic make-up, by our social location, and by countless other scientific parameters. We can be defined by our race, our nationality, our weight, and our gender. Yet all too often, identity is simply reduced to the categories we happen to occupy. The curse of the scientific age is that human beings are reduced to genetic and social stereotypes. Individual identity has become a matter of an impersonal genetic code.

Powerful protests have been raised against this depersonalization of identity. The Jewish philosopher Martin Buber (1878–1965) argued that purely scientific accounts of humanity reduced people to objects: to an "it" rather than a "you." The essence of personal identity, for Buber, is an ability to exist in relationships. We are defined, not by our chemical or genetic make-up, but by our social and personal relationships.[12] Identity is something given, not something achieved. I am given my identity as a father by my children; I am given my identity as a person of significance by the God who has graciously chosen to relate to me and to regard me in this way.

This is a central element of the Christian vision of personal identity and meaning. While the term "soul" is often misunderstood as an immortal component of human identity, its more biblical meaning is "human nature in so far as it relates to God." We find our true identity in our relationship with God, who knows us and gives us our identity and significance. The really important point is this: we do not define ourselves, but we are defined by another, who gives us our identity and significance and safeguards the same. Our identity is not contained in, or safeguarded by, some part of our bodies; it is given and guaranteed by God, who beholds us and remembers us.

Augustine of Hippo made this point in his *Confessions*, written between 397 and 398. Questions of personal identity and significance loom large in this remarkable piece of writing. For Augustine, human destiny and identity are both linked to God, as our creator and redeemer—an idea expressed in Augustine's famous prayer: "You have made us for yourself, and our heart is restless until it finds its rest in you."[13] Human identity is here linked with our intentional origination from God and our subsequent relationship with God, culminating in "finding rest" in God. It is a powerful statement, which suggests a narrative of restoration and homecoming. We are not fully human until we exist in relationship with God. This is a core component of the Christian understanding of human identity.

It's an important point. Many agree that political and social systems ought to enable us to achieve our true humanity. Yet secular humanism argues that religion suppresses human identity, and it concludes that human liberation is dependent upon the suppression of religion. Yet secular humanism seems to ignore the awkward fact that there are multiple narratives of human identity. Its own theory is simply one among many, and it has no claim to special privilege or priority. Many hold that we only achieve our true identity and fulfilment through relating to God. And that vision of human identity has every right to be heard, represented, and enacted in the public sphere.

2. Value: Do I Matter?

One of the most profound pieces of writing in the Old Testament is Psalm 8, which takes the form of reflection on the place of humanity in the natural world. The psalmist considers the immensity of the night sky before turning to consider the place of human beings in this vast universe (8:3–5):

> When I look at your heavens, the work of your fingers,
>   the moon and the stars that you have established;
> what are human beings that you are mindful of them,
>   mortals that you care for them?
> Yet you have made them a little lower than God,
>   and crowned them with glory and honor.

The passage locates humanity between God and the beasts of the field, endowed with dignity on account of their divine creation. The fact that God cares for human beings is seen as being a matter for praise rather than logical analysis. The recognition of God's care for individual human beings precedes our reflections on its theological basis.

God's care for humanity is emphasized throughout the Old Testament. God is our shepherd, who accompanies, supports, and upholds us, even in "the valley of the shadow of death" (Ps. 23 NIV). Yet the New Testament adds a new dimension to this by reaffirming God's love for humanity by linking to the death of Jesus Christ as a tangible demonstration of this commitment and compassion. Paul speaks of this divine commitment at several points: "I live by faith in the Son of God, who loved me and gave himself for me" (Gal. 2:20). The death of Christ is not seen primarily as a biological, or even a judiciary, event; it is interpreted as a token of commitment, a demonstration of God's solidarity with humanity.

Our value thus does not depend upon or reflect our achievements; instead, our value comes in the esteem in which we are held by God. God is our "secure base" (John Bowlby), just as a parent provides the unconditional love and acceptance needed for a child to grow up and learn from mistakes. Such a "secure base" provides a platform for personal growth and maturation and enables us to cope with personal challenges and difficulties. The biblical image of God or the

Christian faith as a "rock" (as in the image of the person who builds their house on a rock rather than on shifting sand: Matt. 7:24–27) expresses these ideas of security and stability in an accessible way. We possess value because we are valued, accepted, and enabled to cope with the challenges of life.

We could speak of the "transvaluation" of human life through being "touched" by God—a theme that is found throughout the poetic writings of George Herbert. In one of his poems, Herbert (1593–1633) likens the graceful "touch" of God to the fabled "philosopher's stone" of medieval alchemy. Just as the philosopher's stone was believed to transmute base metal into gold, so God could transform the value of individuals through grace:

> This is that famous stone
> That turneth all to gold:
> For that which God doth touch and own
> Cannot for less be told.[14]

We are, as the medieval writer Julian of Norwich famously put it, enfolded in the love of Christ, which brings us a new security, identity, and value. Once we see ourselves as enfolded by Christ, we come to think of ourselves in a new way—as those who are valued, welcomed, and loved.

3. Purpose: Why Am I Here?

Purpose is central to serious and meaningful living.[15] On the theory of evolution, one of the more disturbing implications of atheistic interpretations is that we are here by accident, the product of an indifferent cosmic happenstance. This conclusion is not, it must be stressed, demanded by evolutionary biology itself; it is the outcome of fusing the basic themes of evolutionary biology with an aggressive and dogmatic atheism. Yet it is an unsettling thought, even for many atheists who profess to believe it. Some, of course, argue that its metaphysical austerity is an indicator of its truth. When I was an atheist myself, I took a certain pride in believing in such grim and bleak ideas, seeing it as a badge of intellectual courage and integrity.

Bleakness, however, is not an indicator of truth. We might believe that everyone is out to get us, so that life is both pointless and downright dangerous. Yet that conclusion might rest upon our somewhat warped interpretation of the world, rather than the reality of the situation. The Christian answer to this question is grounded in the passionate belief that God chose to enter into human history in the life, death, and resurrection of Jesus Christ—thus enabling us to relate to God, and ultimately to be with God in the new Jerusalem. According to Scripture and the Christian tradition, God is the heart's true desire, the goal of our longings, and the fulfiller of our deepest aspirations. The Christian tradition has developed many ways of expressing this belief. The "chief end" of human existence, according to the Shorter Westminster Catechism (1648), is "to enjoy God, and glorify him for ever." God thus provides a rich and deeply satisfying answer to the profound questions that we ask ourselves about the meaning of life.

The image of a journey helps frame the great questions of purpose in life. Some see life as a random and meaningless process of meandering, in which we search endlessly for a purpose that eludes us, if it exists at all. The Christian tradition sees this journey as having a goal. We walk with a purpose, as we make our way to the new Jerusalem, which is where our true destiny lies. We are, according to the New Testament, "citizens of heaven," who have the right of abode there. Though in exile on earth, our true homeland lies in heaven. God is our shepherd, the one who leads us, guides us, and accompanies us on our way home.

The journey helps us explore the purpose of life from two different perspectives. First, it emphasizes that life has more than just a direction: moving from life to death. It has a goal, a purpose. To be with God is affirmed to be the culmination of all human desires and longings. Everything that is good, beautiful, and true points to God and finds its fulfilment in God. Second, the image of the journey reminds us that we may help others in need along life's road as we travel. Coming home to God and finding rest is the climax of that journey; the process of travelling itself, however, allows us to grow in wisdom and insight and to serve other wayfarers as we travel.

4. Agency: Can I Make a Difference?

Finally, we need to consider an important and often neglected question: Can I make a difference? Or am I so insignificant and powerless that I might as well not be here? The capacity to make a difference with things is seen by many people as integral to their quest for meaning and purpose. *If I cannot make a difference, I might as well not be here*, they think. The issue is that of empowerment. Do we have what it takes to make a difference? Or is this something we need to be enabled to do?

From a Christian perspective, human nature is damaged and wounded by sin, thus not able to achieve its full potential unaided. It is a point made throughout the New Testament, particularly in the writings of Paul. As we noted earlier, Paul was convinced that he was trapped, unable to break free from the prison of his own limitations and weaknesses.[16] What could be done? In the end, Paul found his answer: "Who will rescue me from this body of death? Thanks be to God through Jesus Christ our Lord!" (Rom. 7:24–25).

This theme was particularly developed by Augustine of Hippo, who was exquisitely sensitive to the problem of human weakness, fragility, and brokenness.[17] In Augustine's view, human beings were damaged by sin, which was like a hereditary disease, passed down from one generation to another. Sin weakens humanity and cannot be cured by human agency. Yet Christ is the divine physician, by whose "wounds we are healed" (Isa. 53:5 NIV). We are thus healed by the grace of God, so that our minds may recognize God and our wills may respond to the divine offer of grace.

Or again, Augustine argues that sin is like a power which holds us captive, from whose grip we are unable to break free by ourselves. The human free will is captivated by the power of sin and may only be liberated by grace. Christ is thus seen as the liberator, the source of the grace which breaks the power of sin. Or again, sin is a type of guilt or moral impurity which is passed down from one generation to another. Christ thus comes to bring forgiveness and pardon. Using such images, Augustine builds up a powerful depiction of human nature being weakened, impoverished, and trapped by sin—but healed and liberated by grace.

> The Christian faith does not leave us where we are, while possessing a better understanding of things; it offers to transform our situation.

There is much more that could be said on these themes. The life of faith is to be seen as the divinely enabled pursuit of human aspiration within the recognition of human frailty. It represents an *examined* life, in which each human existence is seen in the mirror of a greater truth and a higher standard. The idea of God's grace gives theological expression to the fundamental Christian experience, hard-wired into the New Testament, that God is one who loves, cares, assists, and maintains a faithful watching presence, even in the darkest and loneliest existential moments. The heart of this life of faith lies not primarily in a set of propositions about reality (although these play an important role), but rather in a trusting orientation and attitude towards God, who is recognized as the sole source of perfection for a being that is clearly intrinsically imperfect. The arrival of God thus brings transformation of our situation, not simply illumination of it.

The all-important point here is that Christianity does not merely enable us to "make sense of things." There is a vast chasm between knowledge and meaning, between information and significance. The Christian faith does not leave us where we are, while possessing a better understanding of things; it offers to transform our situation. It may help us to make sense of our situation if we learn that we are ill, or imprisoned. Yet this knowledge of the true state of things is not in itself transformative. Knowing that we are ill does not automatically lead to healing; it is merely the condition for seeking help. But that help lies to hand. As the traditional African American spiritual puts it:

> There is balm in Gilead,
> to make the wounded whole;
> There's power enough in heaven,
> To cure a sin-sick soul.

Conclusion

*R*ecent atheistic writers have ridiculed the idea of "faith." Only the deliverances of science and reason are to be trusted! For Richard Dawkins, proprietor of the "Richard Dawkins Foundation for Reason and Science," faith "means blind trust, in the absence of evidence, even in the teeth of evidence."[1] It is a powerful piece of rhetoric, whose influence is matched only by its superficiality. The truth is obvious, and it is otherwise. Faith is part of the human condition. It is impossible to construct an argument proving the legitimacy of reason without presupposing faith; the conclusion is implicit in the presupposition. As the great feminist philosopher Julia Kristeva put it so trenchantly and clearly: "Whether I belong to a religion, whether I be agnostic or atheist, when I say 'I believe,' I mean 'I hold as true.'"[2]

To hold that something is true and reliable may be *justified* without necessarily being *proved*. I may have good reasons for believing something to be true, yet realize that I cannot prove this is so. That is just the nature of things. Like Charles Darwin, we might believe that we have developed an excellent theory for making sense of what we observe in the world—but not be able to *prove* it, either to ourselves or to others. Like William Wilberforce, we may believe that slavery is unjust and immoral—but not be able to prove that this is so. Happily, this did not stop Wilberforce and others from pursuing justice.

Christianity may be open to criticism on many grounds, but it is certainly not vulnerable to the charge that, in contrast to scientific or empirical thought, it rests on "mere faith."[3] We must be critical of our beliefs, subjecting them to interrogation. As Paul insists in one of his earliest letters, "test everything; hold fast to what is good"

113

(1 Thess. 5:21). Where Dawkins thinks Christians believe blindly, the New Testament holds them to believe reliably and critically, on the basis of the evidence available.

In this book, we have explored the deep human desire to make sense of things, evident in both the natural sciences and in the Christian faith. We often seem to have a sense of standing on the brink of something greater, lying beyond the horizons of experience and reason. What we do know seems to point beyond itself, to a greater vision of reality. Voices seem to call to us from the ends of the earth, pointing to something deeper and better than anything we presently possess or know. As the poet Matthew Arnold (1822–88) puts it in "The Buried Life":

> Christianity may be open to criticism on many grounds, but it is certainly not vulnerable to the charge that, in contrast to scientific or empirical thought, it rests on "mere faith." We must be critical of our beliefs, subjecting them to interrogation.

> But often, in the world's most crowded streets,
> But often, in the din of strife,
> There rises an unspeakable desire
> After the knowledge of our buried life.

Our engagement with the world awakens a deeper sense of longing, which goes beyond simply making sense of things. We want to be part of something deeper, to be able to be part of a bigger picture.

The Christian way of seeing things makes cognitive and existential sense of reality, offering us a powerful, persuasive, and attractive account of ourselves and our universe. Christianity does not simply make sense *to* us; it also makes sense *of* us. It positions us in the great narrative of cosmic history and locates us on a mental map of meaning. It offers us another way of seeing things, offers us another way of living, and invites us to share these. We need to focus our lives, to have something stable and secure on which we can rest.

It is an important point, famously advocated by Erich Fromm (1900–1980), who was shocked by the insanity and destructiveness of the First World War. He was also distressed by a childhood memory of a young woman who committed suicide shortly after her father's death, unable to cope with life without him. Fromm began to reflect deeply on what people really needed if they were to remain sane. The answer, he argued, lay in developing what he called a "framework of orientation and devotion," a way of thinking about the world which endows existence with purpose and significance. The specific framework that Fromm himself developed is secondary to his recognition that we need such frameworks if we are to live and act in the world without going insane. Living purposefully and meaningfully requires and depends upon a frame of reference, which offers us a secure foundation and focus for our lives.

For Christians, this foundation and focus is the living God, the "God and Father of our Lord Jesus Christ" (2 Cor. 1:3). This God makes himself known in the life, death, and resurrection of Jesus Christ, and in the pages of Scripture. But he also makes something of himself known through the natural world, the world of creation, as a voice which calls us, beckoning from its depths and mysterious beauty.

The great scientist Isaac Newton expressed this feeling perfectly, when he spoke of a greater reality lying beyond and behind what could be observed:

> I seem to have been only like a small boy playing on the sea-shore, diverting myself in now and then finding a smoother pebble or a prettier shell than the ordinary, whilst the great ocean of truth lay all undiscovered before me.[4]

As we walk along the shore of the universe, we take delight in the pebbles and shells we see around us, wondering what they mean. We need to raise our eyes and see the vast ocean of meaning which lies beyond them, and from which they ultimately came. For things of this world are but signs and pointers; and we must let them lead us to their source.

Notes

CHAPTER ONE: LOOKING FOR THE BIG PICTURE

1. Dorothy L. Sayers, *Les origines du roman policier* (Hurstpierpoint, UK: Dorothy L. Sayers Society, 2003).

2. Ibid., 14.

3. William Whewell, *The Philosophy of the Inductive Sciences*, 2 vols. (London: John W. Parker, 1847), 2:36: "The facts are known but they are insulated and unconnected. . . . The pearls are there but they will not hang together until some one provides the string."

4. See Peter R. Dear, *The Intelligibility of Nature: How Science Makes Sense of the World* (Chicago: University of Chicago Press, 2008).

5. Edna St. Vincent Millay, *Collected Sonnets*, rev., exp. ed. (New York: Harper Perennial, 1988), 140.

6. Richard Dawkins, *River out of Eden: A Darwinian View of Life* (London: Phoenix, 1995), 133.

7. Peter B. Medawar, *The Limits of Science* (Oxford: Oxford University Press, 1985), 66.

8. Richard Dawkins, *A Devil's Chaplain: Selected Writings* (London: Weidenfield & Nicolson, 2003), 34.

9. Bertrand Russell, *The Impact of Science upon Society* (London: Routledge, 1998), 97.

CHAPTER TWO: LONGING TO MAKE SENSE OF THINGS

1. Terry Eagleton, *Reason, Faith, and Revolution: Reflections on the God Debate* (New Haven: Yale University Press, 2009), 7.

2. Christopher Hitchens, *God Is Not Great: How Religion Poisons Everything* (New York: Twelve, 2007), 282.

3. William James, *The Will to Believe* (New York: Dover Publications, 1956), 51.

4. Simone Weil, *First and Last Notebooks* (London: Oxford University Press, 1970), 147.

5. The reason for this is that history moves immediately from 1 BC to AD 1, without any intervening year 0.

6. Zygmunt Bauman, "On Writing: On Writing Sociology," *Theory, Culture & Society* 17 (2000): 79–90, with quote from 79.

7. Charles S. Peirce, *Collected Papers*, ed. Charles Hartshorne and Paul Weiss, 8 vols. (Cambridge, MA: Belknap Press of Harvard University Press, 1931–60), 5:189. For further reflection on the notion of "abduction," see Sami Paavola, "Abduction as a Logic of Discovery: The Importance of Strategies," *Foundations of Science* 9 (2005): 267–83; Sami Paavola, "Peircean Abduction: Instinct, or Inference?" *Semiotica* 153 (2005): 131–54.

8. See Michael Polanyi, "Science and Reality," *British Journal for the Philosophy of Science* 18 (1967): 177–96.

9. Isaiah Berlin, *Concepts and Categories: Philosophical Essays* (New York: Viking Press, 1979), 1–11.

10. See esp. Viktor E. Frankl, *Man's Search for Meaning* (New York: Simon & Schuster, 1963).

CHAPTER THREE: PATTERNS ON THE SHORE OF THE UNIVERSE

1. For the history and use of this image, see Clarence J. Glacken, *Traces on the Rhodian Shore: Nature and Culture in Western Thought from Ancient Times to the End of the Eighteenth Century* (Berkeley: University of California Press, 1973).

2. A. F. Alexander, *The Planet Uranus: A History of Observation, Theory and Discovery* (London: Faber & Faber, 1965).

3. Tom Standage, *The Neptune File: A Story of Astronomical Rivalry and the Pioneers of Planet Hunting* (New York: Walker, 2000).

4. Charles Darwin, *On the Origin of Species by Means of Natural Selection*, 6th ed. (London: John Murray, 1872), 444.

5. Charles Darwin, *On the Origin of Species*, 1st ed. (London: John Murray, 1859), 171. For examples of such "difficulties," see Abigail J. Lustig, "Darwin's Difficulties," in *The Cambridge Companion to the "Origin of Species,"* ed. Michael Ruse and Robert J. Richards (Cambridge: Cambridge University Press, 2009), 109–28.

6. For example, Darwin was unable to provide a convincing response to Fleeming Jenkin's concerns about "blending inheritance": see Michael Bulmer, "Did Jenkin's Swamping Argument Invalidate Darwin's Theory of Natural Selection?" *British Journal for the History of Science* 37 (2004): 281–97.

7. For the role of faith in Darwin's scientific and religious reflections, see Alister McGrath, "Religious and Scientific Faith: The Case of Charles Darwin's *The Origin of Species*," in *The Passionate Intellect: Christian Theology and the Discipleship of the Mind* (Downers Grove, IL: InterVarsity Press, 2010), 119–37.

8. William James, "The Sentiment of Rationality," in *The Will to Believe and Other Essays in Popular Philosophy* (New York: Longmans, Green, & Co., 1897), 63–110.

CHAPTER FOUR: HOW WE MAKE SENSE OF THINGS

1. Peter R. Dear, *The Intelligibility of Nature: How Science Makes Sense of the World* (Chicago: University of Chicago Press, 2008), 173.

2. Michael Polanyi, *The Tacit Dimension* (Garden City, NY: Double-day, 1967), 24. See also the more developed approach in C. Stephen Evans, *Natural Signs and Knowledge of God* (Oxford: Oxford University Press, 2010), 26–148.

3. Paul Humphreys, *The Chances of Explanation: Causal Explanation in the Social, Medical, and Physical Sciences* (Princeton, NJ: Princeton University Press, 1989). See also James Woodward, *Making Things Happen: A Theory of Causal Explanation* (Oxford: Oxford University Press, 2003).

4. Paul Thagard, "The Best Explanation: Criteria for Theory Choice," *Journal of Philosophy* 75 (1978): 76–92; Peter Lipton, *Inference to the Best Explanation*, 2nd ed. (London: Routledge, 2004).

5. Michael Friedman, "Explanation and Scientific Understanding," *Journal of Philosophy* 71 (1974): 5–19; Paul Kitcher, "Explanatory Unification and the Causal Structure of the World," in *Scientific Explanation*, ed. P. Kitcher and W. Salmon (Minneapolis: University of Minnesota Press, 1989), 410–505.

6. Robert W. Smith, *The Expanding Universe: Astronomy's "Great Debate," 1900–1931* (Cambridge: Cambridge University Press, 1982); Helge S. Kragh, *Conceptions of Cosmos: From Myths to the Accelerating Universe. A History of Cosmology* (Oxford: Oxford University Press, 2006).

7. Jeremy Bernstein, *Three Degrees above Zero: Bell Laboratories in the Information Age* (New York: Scribner's Sons, 1984).

8. Steven Weinberg, *The First Three Minutes: A Modern View of the Origin of the Universe*, updated ed. (New York: Basic Books, 1993).

9. Some philosophers have argued that the emergence of a quantum particle from a quantum vacuum is an example of something that begins to exist uncaused out of nothing. This, however, rests on a misunderstanding of quantum mechanics: see Alexander Pruss, *The Principle of Sufficient Reason: A Reassessment* (Cambridge: Cambridge University Press, 2006), 160–69.

10. For an introduction to basic Christian understandings of creation, see Alister E. McGrath, *Christian Theology: An Introduction*, 5th ed. (Oxford: Blackwell, 2010), 215–22.

11. William Lane Craig, "In Defense of Theistic Arguments," in *The Future of Atheism*, ed. Robert B. Stewart (Minneapolis: Fortress Press, 2008), 67–96.

12. See Pietro Corsi, *Evolution before Darwin* (Oxford: Oxford University Press, 2011).

13. Charles Darwin, *The Life and Letters of Charles Darwin*, ed. Francis Darwin, 3rd ed., 3 vols. (London: John Murray, 1887), 2:155.

14. John Polkinghorne, *Theology in the Context of Science* (London: SPCK, 2008), 84.

15. Bernard Lonergan, *Insight: A Study of Human Understanding*, 2nd ed. (New York: Philosophical Library, 1958), 684.

CHAPTER FIVE: MUSINGS OF A LAPSED ATHEIST

1. Richard Dawkins, *The God Delusion* (Boston: Houghton Mifflin, 2006); Sam Harris, *The End of Faith: Religion, Terror, and the Future of Reason* (New York: W. W. Norton, 2004); Daniel C. Dennett, *Breaking the Spell: Religion as a Natural Phenomenon* (New York: Viking, 2006); Christopher Hitchens, *God Is Not Great: How Religion Poisons Everything* (New York: Twelve, 2007).

2. Ernest Hemingway, *A Farewell to Arms* (New York: Scribner's, 1997), 13.

3. Ian McEwan, "A Parallel Tradition," *The Guardian*, 1 April 2006, http://www.guardian.co.uk/books/2006/apr/01/scienceandnature.richarddawkins.

4. Tom Wolfe, "The Great Relearning," in *Hooking Up* (London: Jonathan Cape, 2000), 140–45.

5. Richard Dawkins, *A Devil's Chaplain: Selected Writings* (London: Weidenfield & Nicolson, 2003), 16.

6. For a good study, see Michael Stenmark, *Scientism: Science, Ethics and Religion* (Aldershot: Ashgate, 2001).

7. See, e.g., Michael Polanyi, *Personal Knowledge* (New York: Harper & Row, 1964).

8. For its systematic debunking, see Ronald L. Numbers, ed., *Galileo Goes to Jail: And Other Myths about Science and Religion* (Cambridge, MA: Harvard University Press, 2009).

9. Dawkins, *God Delusion,* 66–69.

10. Richard Dawkins, *The Greatest Show on Earth* (London: Transworld, 2009).

11. Dawkins, *God Delusion*, 188.

12. Ibid., 166.

13. On this further, see Gudmundur Ingi Markusson, "Review of *The God Delusion*," *Journal of Cognition and Culture* 7 (2007): 369–73.

14. On this, see Donald E. Brown, *Human Universals* (New York: McGraw-Hill, 1991), 48.

15. Richard Dawkins, *The Selfish Gene*, 2nd ed. (Oxford: Oxford University Press, 1989), 21. I am indebted to Denis Noble for making this point: see esp. Denis Noble, *The Music of Life: Biology beyond the Genome* (Oxford: Oxford University Press, 2006).

16. Samir Okasha, *Evolution and the Levels of Selection* (Oxford: Oxford University Press, 2006), 143–72.

17. Noble, *Music of Life*, 13.

CHAPTER SIX: BEYOND THE SCIENTIFIC HORIZON

1. Thomas H. Huxley, *Darwiniana* (London: Macmillan, 1893), 248–52, with quote from 252.

2. See Thomas H. Huxley, *Collected Essays*, vol. 4 (London: Macmillan, 1895), 139–63.

3. Charles Darwin, *The Life and Letters of Charles Darwin*, ed. Francis Darwin, 3rd ed., 3 vols. (London: John Murray, 1887), 2:200.

4. For what follows, see José Ortega y Gasset, *History as a System and Other Essays toward a Philosophy of History* (New York: W. W. Norton, 1962), 13–15.

5. Richard Dawkins, *A Devil's Chaplain: Selected Writings* (London: Weidenfield & Nicolson, 2003), 37.

6. Charles A. Coulson, *Science and Christian Belief* (Chapel Hill: University of North Carolina Press, 1958), 75.

7. Richard Swinburne, *The Existence of God* (Oxford: Clarendon Press, 1979), 71.

8. On this further, see John Polkinghorne, *One World: The Interaction of Science and Theology* (Princeton, NJ: Princeton University Press, 1986).

9. Albert Einstein, "Physics and Reality," *Journal of the Franklin Institute* 221 (1936): 349–89, with quote from 351.

10. Stephen Jay Gould, "Impeaching a Self-Appointed Judge," *Scientific American* 267, no. 1 (1992): 118–21.

11. For a good popular account and debunking of most of these myths, see Ronald L. Numbers, ed., *Galileo Goes to Jail: And Other Myths about Science and Religion* (Cambridge, MA: Harvard University Press, 2009).

12. M. R. Bennett and P. M. S. Hacker, *Philosophical Foundations of Neuroscience* (Oxford: Blackwell, 2003), 372–76.

13. See, e.g., Maurice Bloch, "A Well-Disposed Social Anthropologist's Problem with Memes," in *Darwinizing Culture: The Status of Memetics as a Science*, ed. Robert Aunger (Oxford: Oxford University Press, 2000), 189–203; Scott Atran, "The Trouble with Memes: Inference versus Imitation in Cultural Creation," *Human Nature* 12 (2001): 351–81; Francisco J. Gil-White, "Common Misunderstandings of Memes (and Genes): The Promise and the Limits of the Genetic Analogy to Cultural Transmission Processes," in *Perspectives on Imitation: From Neuroscience to Social Science*, ed. Susan Hurley and Nick Chater (Cambridge, MA: MIT Press, 2005), 317–38.

14. Richard Dawkins, *The God Delusion* (London: Bantam, 2006), 196.

15. For a detailed analysis of the difficulties, see Liane Gabora, "Ideas Are Not Replicators but Minds Are," *Biology and Philosophy* 19 (2004): 127–43.

16. See the Web site, http://cfpm.org/jom-emit/.

17. Bruce Edmonds, "The Revealed Poverty of the Gene-Meme Analogy— Why Memetics Per Se Has Failed to Produce Substantive Results," online, January 2005, http://cfpm.org/jom-emit/2005/vol9/edmonds_b.html.

CHAPTER SEVEN: A CHRISTIAN VIEWPOINT

1. C. S. Lewis, "Is Theology Poetry?" in *C. S. Lewis: Essay Collection and Other Short Pieces*, ed. Lesley Walmsley (London: HarperCollins, 2000), 1–21, with quote from 21.

2. See, e.g., Ann Loades, "C. S. Lewis: Grief Observed, Rationality Abandoned, Faith Regained," *Literature and Theology* 3 (1989): 107–21; Alister McGrath, "The Cross, Suffering and Theological Bewilderment: Reflections on Martin Luther and C. S. Lewis," in *The Passionate Intellect: Christian Faith and the Discipleship of the Mind* (Downers Grove, IL: InterVarsity Press, 2010), 57–69.

3. For the argument, see Alister E. McGrath, *The Open Secret: A New Vision for Natural Theology* (Oxford: Blackwell, 2008), 115–216.

4. Iris Murdoch, "The Sovereignty of Good over Other Concepts," in *Existentialists and Mystics*, ed. Peter Conradi (London: Chatto, 1998), 363–85, with quote from 368.

5. John Ruskin, *Works*, ed. E. T. Cook and A. Wedderburn, 39 vols. (London: Allen, 1903–12), 5:333.

6. This suggestive phrase was first used by Eugene Wigner, "The Unreasonable Effectiveness of Mathematics," *Communications on Pure and Applied Mathematics* 13 (1960): 1–14.

7. Charles A. Coulson, *Science and Christian Belief* (Chapel Hill: University of North Carolina Press, 1958), 22.

8. Henry Drummond, *The Ascent of Man*, 7th ed. (New York: James Pott, 1897), 334.

9. See John Behr, *Asceticism and Anthropology in Irenaeus and Clement* (Oxford: Oxford University Press, 2000), 34–85; Eric F. Osborn, *Irenaeus of Lyons* (Cambridge: Cambridge University Press, 2001), 51–141.

10. Athanasius, *De incarnatione* 12; also see Khaled Anatolios, *Athanasius* (London: Routledge, 2004), 41–43.

11. John Polkinghorne, *Science and Creation: The Search for Understanding* (London: SPCK, 1988), 20–21; see further idem, *Belief in God in an Age of Science* (New Haven, CT: Yale University Press, 1998).

CHAPTER EIGHT: THE DEEP STRUCTURE OF THE UNIVERSE

1. Martin J. Rees, *New Perspectives in Astrophysical Cosmology*, 2nd ed. (Cambridge: Cambridge University Press, 2000); Edward R. Harrison, *Cosmology: The Science of the Universe*, 2nd ed. (Cambridge: Cambridge University Press, 2000).

2. Ernan McMullin, "Indifference Principle and Anthropic Principle in Cosmology," *Studies in the History and Philosophy of Science* 24 (1993): 359–89.

3. Lee Smolin, *The Life of the Cosmos* (New York: Oxford University Press, 1997), 37.

4. For detailed discussions, see Rodney D. Holder, *God, the Multiverse, and Everything: Modern Cosmology and the Argument from Design* (Aldershot: Ashgate, 2004); Alister E. McGrath, *A Fine-Tuned Universe: The Quest for God in Science and Theology* (Louisville, KY: Westminster John Knox Press, 2009).

5. For philosophical reflection, see Richard Swinburne, "The Argument from the Fine-Tuning of the Universe," in *Physical Cosmology and Philosophy*, ed. John Leslie (New York: Macmillan, 1990), 154–73; Robin Collins, "A Scientific Argument for the Existence of God: The Fine-Tuning Design Argument," in *Reason for the Hope Within*, ed. Michael J. Murray (Grand Rapids: Wm. B. Eerdmans, 1999), 47–75.

6. John Leslie, *Universes* (London: Routledge, 1989), 63.

7. Paul Davies, "The Unreasonable Effectiveness of Science," in *Evidence of Purpose: Scientists Discover the Creator*, ed. John Marks Templeton (New York: Continuum, 1994), 44–56, with quote from 46.

8. C. B. Collins and Stephen Hawking, "Why Is the Universe Isotropic?" *Astrophysical Journal Letters* 180 (1973): 317–34.

9. Brandon Carter, "Large Number Coincidences and the Anthropic Principle," in *Confrontation of Cosmological Theories with Observational Data*, ed. M. S. Longair (Boston: Reidel, 1974), 291–98.

10. John Barrow and Frank J. Tipler, *The Anthropic Cosmological Principle* (Oxford: Oxford University Press, 1986).

11. Jonathan R. Topham, "Biology in the Service of Natural Theology: Darwin, Paley, and the Bridgewater Treatises," in *Biology and Ideology: From Descartes to Dawkins*, ed. Denis R. Alexander and Ronald L. Numbers (Chicago: University of Chicago Press, 2010), 88–113.

12. See, e.g., Paul Davies, *The Goldilocks Enigma: Why Is the Universe Just Right for Life?* (London: Allen Lane, 2006), 147–71.

13. Martin J. Rees, *Just Six Numbers: The Deep Forces That Shape the Universe* (London: Phoenix, 2000), 2–4.

CHAPTER NINE: THE MYSTERY OF THE POSSIBILITY OF LIFE

1. Donald D. Clayton, *Principles of Stellar Evolution and Nucleosynthesis* (New York: McGraw-Hill, 1968).

2. Fred Hoyle, "The Universe: Past and Present Reflections," *Annual Review of Astronomy and Astrophysics* 20 (1982): 1–35, with quote from 16.

3. Bernard J. Carr and Martin J. Rees, "Fine-Tuning in Living Systems," *International Journal of Astrobiology* 3 (2003): 79–86.

4. See esp. R. J. P. Williams and J. J. R. Fraústo da Silva, *The Chemistry of Evolution: The Development of Our Ecosystem* (Boston: Elsevier, 2006); idem, *The Natural Selection of the Chemical Elements: The Environment and Life's Chemistry* (Oxford: Clarendon Press, 1996).

5. Robin Collins, "The Multiverse Hypothesis: A Theistic Perspective," in *Universe or Multiverse?* ed. Bernard Carr (Cambridge: Cambridge University Press, 2007), 459–80.

CHAPTER TEN: THE ACCIDENTS OF BIOLOGICAL HISTORY?

1. See Abigail Lustig, "Natural Atheology," in *Darwinian Heresies*, ed. Abigail Lustig, Robert J. Richards, and Michael Ruse (Cambridge: Cambridge University Press, 2004), 69–83.

2. For a discussion, see the essays in William A. Dembski and Michael Ruse, eds., *Debating Design: From Darwin to DNA* (Cambridge: Cambridge University Press, 2004).

3. As noted by Alister E. McGrath, "The Ideological Uses of Evolutionary Biology in Recent Atheist Apologetics," in *Biology and Ideology: From Descartes to Dawkins*, ed. Denis R. Alexander and Ronald L. Numbers (Chicago: University of Chicago Press, 2010), 329–51. A fuller discussion of this point may be found in Alister E. McGrath, *Darwinism and the Divine: Evolutionary Thought and Natural Theology* (Oxford: Wiley-Blackwell, 2011).

4. For a vigorous statement of this position, see Richard Dawkins, "Darwin Triumphant: Darwinism as Universal Truth," in *A Devil's Chaplain: Selected Writings* (London: Weidenfeld & Nicolson, 2003), 78–90.

5. Thomas H. Huxley, *Lay Sermons, Addresses, and Reviews* (London: Macmillan, 1870), 301.

6. For his complex views on religion, see Sheridan Gilley and Ann Loades, "Thomas Henry Huxley: The War between Science and Religion," *Journal of Religion* 61 (1981): 285–308.

7. Charles Darwin, *The Life and Letters of Charles Darwin*, ed. Francis Darwin, 3rd ed., 3 vols. (London: John Murray, 1887), 2:203–4.

8. See, e.g., Richard Dawkins, *The Blind Watchmaker: Why the Evidence of Evolution Reveals a Universe without Design* (New York: W. W. Norton, 1986). Contrast this with James G. Lennox, "Darwin *Was* a Teleologist," *Biology and Philosophy* 8 (1993): 409–21.

9. Jacques Monod, *Chance and Necessity: An Essay on the Natural Philosophy of Modern Biology* (New York: Alfred A. Knopf, 1971).

10. See esp. Alister E. McGrath, "The Ideological Uses of Evolutionary Biology in Recent Atheist Apologetics," in *Biology and Ideology: From Descartes to Dawkins*, ed. Denis R. Alexander and Ronald L. Numbers (Chicago: University of Chicago Press, 2010), 329–51.

11. Francisco J. Ayala, "Teleological Explanations in Evolutionary Biology," *Philosophy of Science* 37 (1970): 1–15, with quote from 12.

12. Ernst Mayr, *Toward a New Philosophy of Biology: Observations of an Evolutionist* (Cambridge, MA: Harvard University Press, 1988), 38–66.

13. Stephen Jay Gould, *Wonderful Life: The Burgess Shale and the Nature of History* (New York: W. W. Norton, 1989), 290.

14. Simon Conway Morris, *Life's Solution: Inevitable Humans in a Lonely Universe* (Cambridge: Cambridge University Press, 2003), 297.

15. Ibid., 282.

16. Ibid., 144; see the listing of such examples on 457–61.

17. Ibid., 19–21.

18. Simon Conway Morris, "Darwin's Compass: How Evolution Discovers the Song of Creation," *Science and Christian Belief* 18 (2006): 5–22.

19. Francisco J. Ayala, "Intelligent Design: The Original Version," *Theology and Science* 1 (2003): 9–32.

CHAPTER ELEVEN: HISTORY, CULTURE, AND FAITH

1. William Hazlitt, *Essays* (London: Walter Scott, 1889), 269.

2. Proverb 14, contained in Durham Cathedral MS B.III.32. See O. Arngart, "Further Notes on the Durham Proverbs," *English Studies* 58 (1977): 101–4.

3. Terry Eagleton, *Reason, Faith, and Revolution: Reflections on the God Debate* (New Haven, CT: Yale University Press, 2009), 28.

4. See the analysis in Robert J. Louden, *The World We Want: How and Why the Ideals of the Enlightenment Still Elude Us* (Oxford: Oxford University Press, 2007).

5. Christopher Hitchens, *God Is Not Great: How Religion Poisons Everything* (New York: Twelve, 2007), 277–83.

6. Peter Atkins, "Atheism and Science," in *The Oxford Handbook of Religion and Science*, ed. Philip Clayton and Zachary Simpson (Oxford: Oxford University Press, 2006), 136.

7. Daniel Peris, *Storming the Heavens: The Soviet League of the Militant Godless* (Ithaca, NY: Cornell University Press, 1998).

8. Eagleton, *Reason, Faith, and Revolution*, 87–89.

9. J. R. R. Tolkien, "Mythopoeia," in *Tree and Leaf* (London: HarperCollins, 1992), 85–90, with quote from 89.

10. See the famous vision of God's renewed and restored creation in Isa. 2:4: People "shall beat their swords into plowshares, and their spears into pruning hooks; nation shall not lift up sword against nation, neither shall they learn war any more."

11. Louis F. Fieser, "The Synthesis of Vitamin K," *Science* 91 (1940): 31–36.

12. For this and other themes in the debate over the use of the atom bomb, see J. Samuel Walker, "History, Collective Memory, and the Decision to Use the Bomb," *Diplomatic History* 19 (Spring 1995): 319–28.

13. See http://nobelprize.org/nobel_prizes/peace/laureates/1995/rotblat-lecture .html.

14. For this speech—likely as an introduction to the 49th Pugwash Conference on Science and World Affairs, held at Rustenburg, South Africa—see Joseph Rotblat, "Science and Humanity in the Twenty-First Century," 6 September 1999, http:// nobelprize.org/nobel_prizes/peace/laureates/1995/rotblat-article.html?print=1#foot note1.

CHAPTER TWELVE: THE HEART'S DESIRE: LONGING FOR SIGNIFICANCE

1. J. R. R. Tolkien, *Tree and Leaf* (London: HarperCollins, 2001), 87. For the idea in Reformed theology, see Charles Hodge, *Systematic Theology*, 3 vols. (New York: Scribner's, 1917), 1:200. Hodge here argues that God is the true goal of "our religious feelings, our sense of dependence, our consciousness of responsibility [and] our aspirations after fellowship with some Being higher than ourselves, and higher than anything which the world or nature contain."

2. John Paul II, encyclical letter *Fides et Ratio*, 24. Text at http://www.vatican .va/holy_father/john_paul_ii/encyclicals/documents/hf_jp-ii_enc_15101998_fides-et-ratio_en.html.

3. Tolkien, *Tree and Leaf*, 87.

4. Czesław Miłosz, "The Discreet Charm of Nihilism," *New York Times Review of Books*, 19 November 1998, 17–18. For his best and most influential book, see Czesław Miłosz, *The Captive Mind* (New York: Vintage Books, 1981).

5. C. S. Lewis, *Surprised by Joy* (London: Collins, 1989), 138.

6. Richard Dawkins, *River out of Eden: A Darwinian View of Life* (London: Phoenix, 1995), 133.

7. For an assessment of Dawkins's arguments at this point, see Keith Ward, *Why There Almost Certainly Is a God: Doubting Dawkins* (Oxford: Lion Hudson, 2008).

8. For a full discussion, see John Haldane, "Philosophy, the Restless Heart, and the Meaning of Theism," *Ratio* 19 (2006): 421–40.

9. Blaise Pascal, *Pensées* (New York: Penguin, 1995), 45.

10. Here see Verlyn Flieger, *Splintered Light: Logos and Language in Tolkien's World* (Kent, OH: Kent State University Press, 2002), 9–10.

11. Christopher Garbowski, *Recovery and Transcendence for the Contemporary Mythmaker: The Spiritual Dimension in the Works of J. R. R. Tolkien* (Lublin, Poland: Marie Curie-Skłodowska University Press, 2000).

12. Jane Chance, *The Lord of the Rings: The Mythology of Power* (Lexington: University Press of Kentucky, 2001).

13. C. S. Lewis, "Is Theology Poetry?" in *C. S. Lewis: Essay Collection and Other Short Pieces*, ed. Lesley Walmsley (London: HarperCollins, 2000), 1–21, with quote from 15–16.

14. Augustine of Hippo, *Confessions* 1.1.1.

15. C. S. Lewis, "The Weight of Glory," in *Screwtape Proposes a Toast, and Other Pieces* (London: Collins Fontana Books, 1965), 94–110, with quote from 97.

16. Lewis makes significant use of this image in *The Silver Chair*, the sixth of the *Chronicles of Narnia*. See William G. Johnson and Marcia K. Houtman, "Platonic Shadows in C. S. Lewis' Narnia Chronicles," *Modern Fiction Studies* 32 (1986): 75–87.

17. Lewis, "The Weight of Glory," 98–99.

18. Ibid., 106.

CHAPTER THIRTEEN: SURPRISED BY MEANING

1. Pascal, *Pensées*, 19.

2. Ursula Goodenough, *The Sacred Depths of Nature* (Oxford: Oxford University Press, 1998), 10.

3. See further Richard Sorabji, *Emotion and Peace of Mind: From Stoic Agitation to Christian Temptation* (Oxford: Oxford University Press, 2002), 17–54.

4. C. S. Lewis, "Is Theology Poetry?" in *C. S. Lewis: Essay Collection and Other Short Pieces*, ed. Lesley Walmsley (London: HarperCollins, 2000), 1–21, with quote from 21.

5. Roy Baumeister, *Meanings of Life* (New York: Guilford Press, 1991), 29–57.

6. As noted and documented by Richard Weikart, *From Darwin to Hitler: Evolutionary Ethics, Eugenics, and Racism in Germany* (New York: Palgrave Macmillan, 2004).

7. Michael J. Sandel, *Justice: What's the Right Thing to Do?* (New York: Farrar, Straus & Giroux, 2009), 244–69.

8. See, for example, James Schmidt, *What Is Enlightenment? Eighteenth-Century Answers and Twentieth-Century Questions* (Berkeley, CA: University of California Press, 1996).

9. See the analysis in Robert J. Louden, *The World We Want: How and Why the Ideals of the Enlightenment Still Elude Us* (Oxford: Oxford University Press, 2007).

10. See the classic analysis in Alasdair MacIntyre, *Whose Justice? Which Rationality?* (Notre Dame: University of Notre Dame Press, 1988).

11. Michael J. Sandel, *Liberalism and the Limits of Justice* (Cambridge: Cambridge University Press, 1982).

12. Maurice S. Friedman, *Martin Buber: The Life of Dialogue*, 4th ed. (London: Routledge, 2002).

13. Augustine of Hippo, *Confessions* 1.1.1.

14. For a detailed theological commentary on Herbert's *Elixir*, from which this stanza is taken, see Alister McGrath, "The Gospel and the Transformation of Reality: George Herbert's 'Elixir,'" in *The Passionate Intellect: Christian Faith and the Discipleship of the Mind* (Downers Grove, IL: InterVarsity Press, 2010), 45–55.

15. For a classic account of this point, see Rick Warren, *The Purpose-Driven Life: What on Earth Am I Here For?* (Grand Rapids: Zondervan, 2002).

16. Paul writes, e.g., "I can will what is right, but I cannot do it. For I do not do the good I want, but the evil I do not want is what I do" (Rom. 7:18–19).

17. See Alister McGrath, *Heresy: A History of Defending the Truth* (San Francisco: HarperOne, 2009), 159–70.

CONCLUSION

1. Richard Dawkins, *The Selfish Gene*, 2nd ed. (Oxford: Oxford University Press, 1989), 198.

2. Julia Kristeva, *The Incredible Need to Believe* (New York: Columbia University Press, 2009), 3.

3. For an excellent engagement with this point, see Timothy Keller, *The Reason for God: Belief in an Age of Skepticism* (New York: Dutton, 2008), 127–225.

4. David Brewster, *Life of Sir Isaac Newton*, rev. and ed. W. T. Lynn, new ed. (London: William Tegg, 1875), 303.

Index